THE TOKYO SIXTEEN

My maternal grandfather was a member of the resistance during the German occupation of Belgium during the Second World War, enduring arrest and the most horrific experiences in the concentration camps where he was interned. My paternal grandfather, during the First World War, managed to escape captivity. Driven by his deep love for his country, he journeyed through the Netherlands to England and France, rejoining the Belgian troops behind the lines to defend the last remaining part of his homeland.

This book is dedicated to my grandfathers who endured incredibly harsh times during the First and Second World Wars, both on the front lines and in concentration camps. I am convinced that they are part of the Greatest Generation my country has ever known.

Geert Rottiers, Belgium

THE TOKYO SIXTEEN

THE HEROES *of* DOOLITTLE'S RAID ON JAPAN *in* APRIL 1942

GEERT ROTTIERS

THE TOKYO SIXTEEN
The Heroes of Doolittle's Raid on Japan in April 1942

First published in Great Britain in 2025 by
Air World
An imprint of
Pen & Sword Books Ltd
Yorkshire – Philadelphia

Copyright © Geert Rottiers, 2025

ISBN 978 1 03613 438 9

The right of Geert Rottiers to be identified as Author of this work has been asserted by him in accordance with the Copyright, Designs and Patents Act 1988.

A CIP catalogue record for this book is available from the British Library.

All rights reserved. No part of this book may be reproduced, transmitted, downloaded, decompiled or reverse engineered in any form or by any means, electronic or mechanical including photocopying, recording or by any information storage and retrieval system, without permission from the Publisher in writing. NO AI TRAINING: Without in any way limiting the Author's and Publisher's exclusive rights under copyright, any use of this publication to "train" generative artificial intelligence (AI) technologies to generate text is expressly prohibited. The Author and Publisher reserve all rights to license uses of this work for generative AI training and development of machine learning language models.

Typeset by SJmagic DESIGN SERVICES, India.

Printed and bound in the UK by CPI Group (UK) Ltd.

The Publisher's authorised representative in the EU for product safety is Authorised Rep Compliance Ltd., Ground Floor, 71 Lower Baggot Street, Dublin D02 P593, Ireland. www.arccompliance.com

For a complete list of Pen & Sword titles please contact

PEN & SWORD BOOKS LIMITED
George House, Units 12 & 13, Beevor Street, Off Pontefract Road,
Barnsley, South Yorkshire, S71 1HN, England
E-mail: enquiries@pen-and-sword.co.uk
Website: www.pen-and-sword.co.uk

or
PEN AND SWORD BOOKS
1950 Lawrence Rd, Havertown, PA 19083, USA
E-mail: uspen-and-sword@casematepublishers.com
Website: www.penandswordbooks.com

Contents

Introduction vi

General James H. Doolittle 1
Colonel Travis Hoover 17
Captain Robert M. Gray 29
Brigadier General Everett W. Holstrom 45
Major General David M. Jones 57
Lieutenant Dean E. Hallmark 70
Major Ted W. Lawson Jr. 89
Colonel Edward J. York 102
Lieutenant Colonel Harold F. Watson 113
Lieutenant Colonel Richard O. Joyce 124
Colonel Charles R. Greening 134
Colonel William M. Bower 148
Lieutenant Colonel Edgar E. McElroy 161
Brigadier General John A. Hilger 171
Captain Donald G. Smith 182
Lieutenant William G. Farrow 195

Sources 206

Introduction

The Tokyo Sixteen: *The Heroes of Doolittle's Raid On Japan in April 1942* is a heart-pounding and gripping account of the lives of sixteen pilots who made history during the daring Doolittle Raid on Tokyo in April 1942. Each chapter of this book vividly brings one of these heroes to life, taking the reader on a thrilling journey through their personal stories, from their youth to their audacious participation in one of the most perilous military missions of World War II.

But the story doesn't stop with the raid itself; it reaches into the post-raid and post-World War II era, examining the profound impact the mission had on each pilot's life. The book delves deep into their experiences after the raid, exploring how they adjusted to life after the war and the various challenges they faced as they moved forward from this defining moment in history. *The Tokyo Sixteen* is more than just a recounting of a bold wartime operation; it stands as a tribute to the courage, resilience, and enduring legacy of Doolittle's brave pilots.

The story begins with an in-depth exploration of the youth and backgrounds of each of the sixteen pilots. These men hailed from different corners of America, each with unique dreams and ambitions, but all united by a shared sense of duty and patriotism. Each biographical portrait reveals the motivations that drove them to join the military and ultimately volunteer for a mission that would take them deep into enemy territory.

The tension mounts as the biographies transition into the secretive and grueling training that preceded the raid. Each pilot faced immense challenges as they prepared for the seemingly impossible: launching heavy B-25 bombers from an aircraft carrier, a technical feat that had never been attempted before. The intensity of this preparation, the fear of failure, and the camaraderie that developed among the pilots are described with electrifying suspense, keeping the reader on the edge of their seat.

But the real action begins when the raid itself unfolds. The biographies offer an unparalleled look at the nerve-wracking moments as these sixteen men took off from the USS *Hornet*, uncertain if they would survive their mission. The book highlights the courageous decisions each pilot had to make as they flew through hostile airspace, dropped bombs on strategic targets in Tokyo, and then had to find their way to safety. These personal tales of bravery and survival form the heart of The Tokyo Sixteen, each one as thrilling and captivating as the next.

The aftermath of the raid is no less compelling. Some of the pilots crash-landed in enemy territory or in the East Chinese Sea, while others found their way back to friendly ground, often with death at their heels. Each chapter concludes with a powerful account of the physical and mental scars left by the raid, and how these experiences shaped the rest of their lives.

The Tokyo Sixteen concludes with a powerful reflection on the enduring legacy of these men. By following their personal biographies, readers gain a deeper understanding of what it truly means to be a hero. This book is a tribute to their unwavering courage, their determination to achieve the impossible, and their lasting impact on history. Their stories are not only thrilling but also inspiring – a reminder of the strength of the human spirit in the most extreme circumstances.

A special website accompanies the book, offering additional resources, including detailed maps, texts, crew rosters, and technical background information: https://www.doolittle-raid.net.

There is a link to the author's Facebook page dedicated to the Doolittle Raid, which (as of writing) has over 46,000 engaged followers and is still growing day by day. This provides direct access to a highly interested audience passionate about this historical event.

List of the sixteen pilots and the respective crews they belonged to during the Doolittle Raid.

Crew 1: Lieutenant Colonel James H. Doolittle
Crew 2: Lieutenant Travis Hoover
Crew 3: Lieutenant Robert M. Gray
Crew 4: Lieutenant Everett W. Holstrom
Crew 5: Captain David M. Jones
Crew 6: Lieutenant Dean E. Hallmark
Crew 7: Lieutenant Ted W. Lawson
Crew 8: Captain Edward J. York
Crew 9: Lieutenant Harold F. Watson
Crew 10: Lieutenant Richard O. Joyce
Crew 11: Captain Charles R. Greening
Crew 12: Lieutenant William M. Bower
Crew 13: Lieutenant Edgar E. McElroy
Crew 14: Major John A. Hilger
Crew 15: Lieutenant Donald G. Smith
Crew 16: Lieutenant William G. Farrow

Note: The ranks mentioned above reflect the military ranks held by the pilots during the Doolittle Raid.

These men flew the perilous mission knowing they likely wouldn't be able to return to the carrier that launched them. The B-25 bombers were loaded with fuel and bombs, making the takeoff from the USS *Hornet* particularly challenging. Some crews were captured by the Japanese, and others were helped by Chinese civilians. Despite the challenges, the raid was a significant morale boost for the United States and had a lasting impact on the war in the Pacific.

Four of the pilots did not survive the war. Lieutenant Dean E. Hallmark (Crew 6) and Lieutenant William G. Farrow (Crew 16) were executed by the Japanese on 15 October 1942, after being captured. Lieutenant Robert M. Gray (Crew 3) and Lieutenant Donald G. Smith (Crew 15) died in aircraft crashes during the war.

These brave men sacrificed their lives in the fight for freedom, and their courageous actions, flying the B-25 bombers in one of the most daring raids of the Second World War, remain an important reminder of the sacrifices made during the conflict.

Geert Rottiers, Belgium

Pilot of Crew 1 and Mission Leader of the Doolittle Raid

General James H. Doolittle

James Harold Doolittle, commonly known as Jimmy Doolittle, was born on 14 December 1896, in Alameda, California. Jimmy Doolittle grew up in a working-class family. His father, Frank Henry Doolittle, was a carpenter and gold prospector, and his mother, Rosa Cerenah Shephard, was a homemaker. The family moved frequently due to his father's search for gold, which took them to Alaska during Jimmy's early years. This exposure to the rugged, adventurous lifestyle in Alaska played a significant role in shaping his daring spirit. Both his parents, Frank and Rosa, hailed from the Midwest – Frank from Michigan and Rosa from Missouri. Their marriage was rooted in a spirit of adventure, a quality that would greatly influence their son. This pioneering spirit would later propel Jimmy to become one of the most daring and innovative aviators in American history.

During his early years, Jimmy lived in Nome, Alaska, where his father pursued the promise of gold during the "rush". Life in Alaska was fraught with challenges, including harsh weather and financial instability. Frank's ventures in gold mining were not always successful, and the family endured tough times.

Despite these difficulties, Jimmy's mother remained a steadying force in his life. She instilled in him a strong desire to learn and an unyielding determination to overcome obstacles, traits that would define his future career. Jimmy Doolittle was known for his curiosity and mechanical aptitude from a young age. He attended school in Nome, Alaska, where he developed an interest in engineering and mechanics.

In 1908, when Jimmy was 12 years old, the Doolittle family relocated to California, settling in Los Angeles. It was in this environment that he began to excel academically and athletically. He attended Manual Arts High School, where he became known for his athletic abilities, particularly in gymnastics and boxing. His physical prowess earned him a reputation as a tough and resilient young man – qualities that would later serve him well in his military career.

Jimmy's first exposure to flight came in 1910, when his school attended the Los Angeles International Air Meet at Dominguez Field and Jimmy saw his first airplane. This experience captivated him and planted the seeds for his lifelong fascination with aviation. He would later recall the excitement of seeing those early airplanes and knowing immediately that he wanted to fly. This fascination grew stronger as he witnessed the development of aviation technology in the years leading up to the First World War.

After witnessing the air show, Jimmy became more attuned to the burgeoning field of aviation. He avidly followed the news and developments in the field, reading about the accomplishments of pioneering aviators such as Glenn Curtiss, Louis Blériot, and the Wright brothers. These figures became his heroes, and he studied their techniques and innovations closely. Jimmy was particularly intrigued by the technological challenges of flight, such as engine performance, aerodynamics and aircraft stability, areas that would later become his specialties.

His growing interest led him to seek out any opportunity to be near airplanes. He spent time at local airfields, where he could observe the mechanics at work and talk to pilots and ground crew. Even as a teenager, Jimmy was known for asking insightful questions about the technical aspects of flying and aircraft maintenance. This hands-on exposure further deepened his understanding of aviation technology and sharpened his desire to become a pilot himself.

During his teenage years, Jimmy's fascination with flight was further fueled by the achievements of the aviation pioneers he admired. He was particularly inspired by the story of Louis Blériot, who had made the first flight across the English Channel in 1909, and by the Wright brothers' continuous advancements in flight control and aircraft design. These accomplishments made him believe there were no limits to what could be achieved in the field of aviation, and he wanted to be at the forefront of these advancements.

After high school, Jimmy enrolled at Los Angeles Junior College, but his time there was brief. It was during this period that his fascination with aviation really began to take flight. He enrolled at the University of California, Berkeley, where he pursued studies in the College of Mines. He became a member of the Theta Kappa Nu fraternity.

In 1917, with the United States entering the First World War, Jimmy Doolittle left his studies to enlist in the Army Signal Corps Reserve as a flying cadet. He completed his flight training at the School of Military Aeronautics at the University of California, Berkeley, and Rockwell Field in California. By March 1918, Jimmy had earned his commission as a lieutenant, quickly establishing himself as a skilled and fearless pilot. Although his combat experience during the First World War was limited, mainly serving as a flight instructor, his post-war career was marked by groundbreaking contributions to aviation.

On 24 December 1917, in the same year that he embarked on his military aviation career, Jimmy Doolittle married Josephine "Joe" Daniels, in Los Angeles, where they had met. Their marriage was characterized by deep affection and mutual support. Josephine was a constant source of strength for Jimmy, providing unwavering encouragement throughout the many challenges and successes of his career. The couple went on to have two sons, James Jr. and John, both of whom followed in their father's footsteps by serving in the military. The Doolittle family was close-knit, with Josephine playing a key role in maintaining stability at home while Jimmy pursued his demanding and often dangerous career.

Before the Second World War, Jimmy's aviation career was defined by a series of pioneering achievements that significantly advanced the field of aviation. His work as a test pilot, his contributions to aeronautical engineering, and his record-setting flights made him one of the most respected and influential figures in aviation during the interwar period.

In 1922, Jimmy made one of his most notable achievements: the first successful transcontinental flight across the United States in under twenty-four hours. Flying a de Havilland DH-4 biplane, he covered the distance from Pablo Beach, Florida, to Rockwell Field, California, with only one stop in San Antonio, Texas. This remarkable feat showcased not only his exceptional piloting skills but also the potential for long-distance air travel, which was still in its early stages.

In addition to his long-distance flights, Jimmy became renowned for his expertise in aerobatics and precision flying. In 1925, he won the prestigious Schneider Trophy, an international seaplane race, flying a Curtiss R3C-2. His victory brought significant attention to American aviation and demonstrated the competitive potential of U.S. aircraft on the global stage. Perhaps one of his most significant contributions to aviation during this period was his pioneering work in advancing instrument flying.

In the early days of aviation, pilots relied heavily on visual cues to navigate, which posed serious risks in poor weather or nighttime conditions. Recognizing the dangers of "blind" flying, Jimmy collaborated with the Guggenheim Fund for the Promotion of Aeronautics to develop and demonstrate the feasibility of instrument flying. In 1929, Jimmy made history by conducting the first-ever "blind" flight, in which he took off, flew, and landed a plane using only instruments. This groundbreaking flight took place at Mitchel Field in New York, where Jimmy used a specially designed hood to block his view outside the cockpit. He relied entirely on instruments such as a barometric altimeter, directional gyroscope, and artificial horizon – devices that have since become standard in all aircraft. This achievement revolutionized aviation by proving that pilots could safely fly without visual references, paving the way for all-weather and night flying.

In 1930, Jimmy initially left active duty in the U.S. Army Air Corps after establishing himself as one of the most skilled pilots and innovative minds in aviation. He transitioned to a civilian role, joining the Shell Oil Company as a manager of aviation and later as a vice president. In this capacity, Jimmy was instrumental in promoting the development of high-octane aviation gasoline, which significantly enhanced aircraft performance, particularly for military aircraft. His work with Shell not only benefited commercial aviation but also had far-reaching implications for military aviation as the world moved closer to another global conflict.

As global tensions escalated in the late 1930s, Jimmy re-entered active military service in 1940, as the U.S. prepared for the possibility of entering the Second World War. His extensive experience, technical expertise, and leadership skills made him an invaluable asset to the military, and he was soon given significant responsibilities as the war approached. Recognizing the need for experienced leaders in the rapidly modernizing U.S. Army Air Corps (which would become the U.S. Army Air Forces in 1941), Jimmy left his civilian position and rejoined the military with the rank of major. His technical expertise, leadership abilities, and reputation as an innovative thinker made him a key figure as the military expanded and modernized in anticipation of the conflict.

In 1940, Major Doolittle's initial responsibilities included overseeing the transition of civilian aviation technology and techniques into the military, with a particular focus on the development and use of high-octane aviation fuel. His efforts were crucial in improving the performance of military aircraft, especially the high-performance fighters and bombers that would play a critical role in the coming war. Jimmy's return to the military also saw him take on roles related to the training and organization of air units. His experience as both a test pilot and an engineer allowed him to contribute significantly to the preparation of the U.S. Army Air Forces, ensuring that air units were equipped with the latest technology and tactics.

As the United States moved closer to entering the Second World War, Jimmy's reputation and expertise positioned him for greater responsibilities. By the end of 1940, he was on the path to becoming one of the key figures in U.S. air strategy. In 1941, his role within the U.S. Army Air Corps became increasingly prominent as the United States prepared for the possibility of entering the Second World War.

During 1941, Major Doolittle leveraged his extensive experience in aviation, focusing on several key areas:

1. **Technical Development and Aviation Fuel:** Jimmy's engineering background and work with Shell Oil Company made him a leading authority on high-octane aviation fuel. Throughout 1941, he played a pivotal role in ensuring that U.S. military aircraft

were equipped with the most advanced fuel available, essential for maximizing the performance of the new generation of high-speed fighters and bombers. His contributions helped prepare the U.S. Army Air Forces to face the advanced aircraft used by Axis powers.

2. **Training and Organization:** As the U.S. military rapidly expanded in response to the growing global conflict, Jimmy was involved in the training and organization of air units. His experience as a test pilot and his understanding of aviation technology made him an ideal leader for overseeing the preparation of pilots and aircrews. Jimmy's work ensured that the Army Air Forces were better prepared for the challenges they would soon face in combat.
3. **Planning for Offensive Operations:** By 1941, Jimmy was also involved in the early planning stages of what would later become the 'Doolittle Raid' on Tokyo. Although the raid itself did not take place until April 1942, the groundwork for this audacious operation began in the latter half of 1941. Jimmy's expertise in both long-distance flight and tactical innovation made him the natural choice to lead this mission. The planning involved considering the feasibility of launching B-25 bombers from an aircraft carrier – an unprecedented idea that required careful preparation and training.
4. **Liaison and Coordination:** In 1941, Jimmy also served as a liaison between the military and various civilian industries, particularly those involved in aircraft production and technological development. His ability to bridge the gap between the military and the private sector helped accelerate the production and deployment of advanced aircraft and other essential war materials.

As 1941 progressed, the attack on Pearl Harbor on 7 December 1941, brought the United States fully into the Second World War.

This event dramatically shifted the focus of Major Doolittle's work from preparation and planning to active combat operations. In the immediate aftermath of Pearl Harbor, Jimmy intensified his efforts to prepare for a retaliatory strike against Japan, which would culminate in the historic Doolittle Raid.

By the end of 1941, Jimmy was firmly established as one of the key leaders in the U.S. Army Air Forces, poised to make significant contributions to the Allied war effort. His work throughout the year laid the foundation for some of the most audacious and innovative operations of the Second World War, demonstrating his unique combination of technical expertise, leadership, and bold thinking.

The Doolittle Raid, officially known as the Tokyo Raid, was one of the most daring and impactful operations of the Second World War. Taking place on 18 April 1942, this mission came just a few months after the devastating attack on Pearl Harbor, marking a critical point early in the United States' involvement in the war. The raid was conceived as a bold and creative response to the Japanese aggression, aiming to deliver a psychological blow to Japan by striking directly at its capital and other key cities. It was designed not only to damage Japanese morale but also to boost American spirits by proving that Japan was vulnerable to American air attacks.

The operation involved launching sixteen B-25 Mitchell bombers from the USS *Hornet*, an aircraft carrier positioned in the Pacific Ocean. This was a highly unorthodox and risky maneuver, as it was the first time medium bombers had ever been launched from a carrier, a feat that required meticulous planning and careful training. The raid targeted several major cities, including Tokyo, Yokohama, Kobe, Nagoya, and Osaka, hitting military installations and industrial sites. Although the material damage inflicted was relatively minor, the raid's psychological impact was enormous, as it shocked the

Japanese leadership and forced them to divert resources to protect their home islands, altering their strategic calculations.

The Doolittle Raid also served as a critical morale booster for the United States. It demonstrated American resolve and capability, helping to galvanize the nation's war effort and rally support among the Allied forces. Moreover, the raid showcased the potential of carrier-based airpower and set the stage for future U.S. naval operations in the Pacific, contributing significantly to the eventual Allied victory in the theater.

The idea for the Doolittle Raid originated within the higher echelons of the U.S. military, particularly the Navy and Army Air Forces, which considered the possibility of launching medium bombers from an aircraft carrier to strike targets in Japan. Lieutenant Colonel Doolittle, who by this time was already a respected figure in aviation and the military, was selected to plan and lead the mission. His experience as a pilot, engineer, and leader made him an ideal choice for this high-risk operation. His plan involved using B-25 Mitchell bombers, which he calculated were light enough to take off from an aircraft carrier but still capable of carrying a significant bomb load to Japan.

Jimmy and his team of volunteers underwent intensive and specialized training to prepare for the mission. The training took place at Eglin Field in Florida and focused on short takeoffs, low-altitude flying, and bombing techniques. Preparing for the Doolittle Raid was a complex and highly secretive process; the pilots learned how to launch their B-25s from the short deck of an aircraft carrier, which required mastering takeoffs in just 500 feet – far less than what was normally required.

Lieutenant Doolittle and his team had to address several key challenges:

1. **Aircraft Modification:** The B-25s needed to be modified to meet the mission's specific requirements. The planes were

stripped of unnecessary equipment to reduce weight, which allowed them to carry more fuel. Additional fuel tanks were installed to extend their range, and bomb bay fuel tanks were added. The bombers were also fitted with modified carburetors to improve fuel efficiency. Defensive armament was minimized, with tail guns replaced by mock guns made of broomsticks to save weight.

2. **Carrier Launch Feasibility:** One of the most critical aspects of the raid was proving that the B-25s could take off from an aircraft carrier's short deck. To accomplish this, Jimmy oversaw a series of test flights in which pilots practiced short takeoffs using a painted runway that simulated the deck of a carrier. As noted, the pilots had to learn to get the B-25 airborne within just 500 feet – a challenging task, especially when fully loaded with bombs and fuel.
3. **Crew Selection and Training:** Jimmy needed highly skilled and motivated volunteers for this mission. The crews were handpicked from the 17th Bombardment Group, known for its proficiency with the B-25. These men were sworn to secrecy and underwent rigorous training. The training regimen included short takeoff drills, low-altitude flying, navigation over long distances without visual landmarks, and bomb aiming under simulated combat conditions. The pilots practiced repeatedly until they could perform the necessary maneuvers with precision.
4. **Coordination with the Navy:** The operation required close coordination with the U.S. Navy, which would provide the carriers and escort ships. The USS *Hornet* was chosen to carry the bombers. The Navy worked with Jimmy to ensure that the launch could be executed safely and efficiently. Both services coordinated on the timing of the launch, the route to Japan, and contingency plans for recovery after the mission.

5. **Secrecy and Deception:** Given the unprecedented nature of the raid and the high stakes involved, maintaining secrecy was paramount. The entire operation was kept under wraps, with details disclosed only to those directly involved. The task force, which included the USS *Hornet* and its escort ships, departed from San Francisco under strict radio silence. The crews themselves were only informed of their specific targets once they were already at sea, minimizing the risk of leaks.

As the launch date approached, Lieutenant Colonel Doolittle and his men finalized their preparations aboard the USS *Hornet*. On 2 April 1942, the task force left San Francisco, heading toward Japan. The crews used the time at sea to review their mission plans, practice their bombing techniques, and mentally prepare for the challenges ahead. However, the mission's complexities did not end with the takeoff. The plan required the bombers to fly over Japan, drop their bombs, and then continue westward to reach airfields in China. The distance was already at the edge of the B-25s' operational range, and any deviation or unexpected event could jeopardize their chances of reaching safety.

On 18 April 1942, the task force was spotted by a Japanese picket boat, forcing an early launch. The bombers took off from the *Hornet* approximately 650 miles from Japan. Despite this setback, Jimmy – mission leader and pilot of Crew 1 – gave the order to proceed, understanding the increased risk but determined to carry out the mission. Jimmy was the first to take off, leading the formation of sixteen B-25 bombers toward Japan. The launch was a remarkable achievement in itself, as the planes lifted off the carrier deck in rough seas – something that had never been done before.

Jimmy's plane took off from the USS *Hornet* at 8:20 am on 18 April 1942, identified by its USAAF serial number 40-2344 and

NAA manufacturer's serial number 62B-3013. The plane did not have a designated name.

The sixteen bombers successfully reached their targets, striking military and industrial sites in Tokyo, Yokohama, Kobe, Nagoya, and Osaka. The crews then faced a perilous journey to China, where they hoped to land safely. Due to the early launch and fuel constraints, most of the bombers either crash-landed or the crews bailed out over China. One plane flew towards Russia and landed near Vladivostok.

Because they had taken off from the *Hornet* earlier than planned, the B-25 bombers faced a severe fuel shortage. After bailing out above China, Jimmy and his crew were scattered across the region, but they eventually regrouped with the help of Chinese civilians and resistance fighters who guided them to safety.

Because large parts of China were occupied by Japan, and despite the challenging terrain and the presence of Japanese forces, Jimmy and his crew members were able to evade capture and eventually made their way to friendly Chinese territory. Their safe return was a remarkable testament to the bravery of the Chinese people who assisted them and the resilience of the Doolittle Raiders.

Upon arriving in Chongqing, the capital of Free China, Jimmy and his men were debriefed by American and Chinese officials. The Chinese Nationalist government, led by Chiang Kai-shek, was grateful for the raid against Japan, which had been a significant morale boost for the Chinese as well as the Americans.

After the raid, Jimmy and some of his crew members made their way from China through various routes, including stops in India and the Middle East, before finally returning to the United States. Jimmy himself feared that the mission had been a failure due to the loss of all the aircraft and the difficulties faced by the crews. However, he was greeted as a national hero upon his return to the U.S., and in June 1942 he was awarded the Medal of Honor by President Franklin D. Roosevelt for his leadership and bravery during the raid. The citation for the Medal of Honor praised Lieutenant Colonel Doolittle's "conspicuous leadership above and beyond the call of duty, involving personal valor and intrepidity at an extreme hazard to life."

Jimmy's return to the U.S. marked the beginning of the next phase of his military career, where he continued to serve in increasingly significant roles throughout the Second World War. His career continued to progress significantly, as he took on important roles in the U.S. military and made major contributions to the Allied effort. Following the raid, Jimmy was promoted from lieutenant colonel to brigadier general, skipping the rank of full colonel, as a recognition of the significance of his accomplishment.

Jimmy was then assigned to command the 12th Air Force in North Africa in November 1942. In this role, he played a key part in Operation Torch, the Allied invasion of North Africa, helping to coordinate air operations that were crucial to the success of the campaign. His leadership in integrating strategic bombing, close air support, and tactical air operations was instrumental in the Allies' victories in the Mediterranean.

In November 1943, he took command of the 15th Air Force, which was responsible for strategic bombing missions against targets in Italy, Germany, and the Balkans. His efforts in this role helped disrupt Axis supply lines and weaken their industrial capabilities, contributing to the broader Allied strategy in Europe.

In January 1944, he was promoted to lieutenant general and took command of the 8th Air Force, the largest and most powerful Air Force in the world at the time. Based in England, the 8th Air Force was central to the strategic bombing campaign against Nazi Germany. General Doolittle made a significant decision to use fighter escorts to protect bombers all the way to and from their targets, rather than just near the bombers. This strategy, especially using P-51 Mustang fighters, played a key role in achieving air superiority over Europe and reducing bomber losses.

After the Second World War, Jimmy continued to play a pivotal role in shaping the future of aviation and aerospace technology. His extensive experience and forward-thinking mindset made him a valuable asset in the post-war period, particularly during the critical years after 1947, when the U.S. Air Force was being established as a separate branch of the military. Jimmy's expertise was instrumental in defining the strategic direction of the new Air Force, especially regarding advancements in jet propulsion and long-range bombing capabilities, which were vital during the early years of the Cold War.

Beyond his military contributions, Jimmy also made significant strides in the burgeoning field of space exploration. He was deeply involved in early discussions and planning that would lay the groundwork for the United States' entry into the Space Race. His advocacy for research into high-speed flight, rocketry, and atmospheric re-entry techniques was crucial in the development of technologies that would later be used in both manned and unmanned space missions.

In the commercial aviation sector, Jimmy's influence extended to several aerospace companies, where he served in advisory roles. His insights were sought after for the development of new commercial aircraft designs that would revolutionize air travel, making it faster, safer, and more efficient. His efforts in promoting innovations in aviation fuel, navigation systems, and aircraft safety standards had lasting impacts on both military and civilian aviation. Jimmy's legacy in the post-war years was one of visionary leadership, bridging the gap between military necessity and technological innovation, helping to propel the United States into a new era of aviation and space exploration.

James Harold "Jimmy" Doolittle's enduring legacy is firmly rooted in the extraordinary contributions he made to aviation and military strategy, which continue to resonate across the generations. His approach to flight, including his pioneering efforts in developing instrument flying and high-speed aviation techniques, fundamentally transformed both military and civilian aviation. These advancements not only improved the safety and effectiveness of aerial operations but also laid the groundwork for modern flight practices used today.

Jimmy's leadership during the Second World War, particularly in the Doolittle Raid, has become a benchmark of strategic innovation and bravery. His ability to inspire and lead under challenging circumstances demonstrated exceptional courage and tactical brilliance, qualities that have made him a lasting symbol of American resilience. His story is frequently studied in military academies, serving as an educational tool and an inspirational tale for those pursuing careers in service to their country.

James Harold Doolittle passed away on 27 September 1993, at the age of 96. His burial at Arlington was a fitting tribute to his remarkable life and service to his country. The ceremony reflected the profound respect and gratitude of a nation that remembered him not only for his leadership during the Second World War, but also for his extensive contributions to aviation and military strategy. As a Medal of Honor recipient, his burial included all the honors befitting a military hero, including a ceremonial flyover by aircraft from the U.S. Air Force, a gun salute, and the folding and presentation of the American flag to his family.

His gravesite is located among those of other prominent military figures, ensuring that he rests in the company of fellow heroes who also served the United States with distinction. Visitors to Arlington National Cemetery can pay their respects to Doolittle and reflect on his significant contributions to the fields of aviation and military strategy. His place at Arlington stands as a lasting reminder of his courage, innovation, and dedication to his country, qualities that continue to inspire generations of military leaders and aviators.

Pilot of Crew 2

Colonel Travis Hoover

Colonel Travis Wayne Hoover's story begins in the small rural town of Melrose, New Mexico, where he was born on 21 September 1917. His parents, John Fredrick Hoover and Irie Elizabeth Threewit, were hardworking individuals who instilled the values of diligence, integrity, and patriotism in their children. Melrose, a modest town nestled in the expansive landscapes of eastern New Mexico, was a place defined by its tight-knit community and the simple, yet profound, lessons it offered its young residents. For Travis, the town's lack of modern luxuries was more than compensated by the richness of community life and the opportunities to develop a strong sense of responsibility and resilience.

His father Fred was a farmer, which was not uncommon for the rural character of New Mexico at the time. He grew up in an environment where hard work was a central part of life. As a farmer in the early twentieth century, Fred likely managed the land and provided for the family through farming, a typical livelihood in agricultural communities of the region.

Lizzie, his mother, was the nurturing force in the family. She oversaw the household and played a key role in raising Travis and his brother and sister. Travis was the youngest of three. At that time, it was common for mothers to take care of the home, ensure the wellbeing of their children, and instill the values and discipline necessary for their future lives.

Travis Hoover's upbringing in this rural, hardworking environment likely shaped his character and work ethic, traits that would serve him well in his military career. The support of both his father and mother probably provided a strong foundation for his later success as a pilot, especially in the challenging circumstances of the Doolittle Raid.

Travis's early education took place in the local elementary school, a modest institution typical of rural America in the early twentieth century. The school focused on providing a solid foundation in basic subjects like reading, writing, and arithmetic. However, much of his learning occurred outside the classroom as well. In a community where everyone knew one another, education extended beyond textbooks; it was embedded in the everyday interactions and experiences of life in a small town. Stories of hardship, perseverance, and triumph shared by the townspeople greatly influenced Travis. These formative years in Melrose, surrounded by individuals who faced life's challenges with determination, fostered in him a deep appreciation for perseverance, a quality that would become a defining characteristic of his life.

In the early 1930s, the Hoover family decided to leave Melrose in search of better opportunities and relocated to Riverside, California. This move was a significant turning point for Travis. Riverside, a rapidly growing community in Southern California, offered a stark contrast to the rural simplicity of Melrose. It was a place of greater possibilities, where a young man like Travis could dream bigger and aim higher. Here, Travis enrolled at Riverside Polytechnic High School, commonly known as "Poly High." The school was known for its strong academic programs and its emphasis on preparing students for higher education and practical careers.

At Poly High, Travis blossomed. He was more than just a student; he was an active participant in various extracurricular activities, which helped him develop leadership skills, a sense of teamwork, and the discipline that would later be essential in his military career. These high school years were pivotal, shaping the young man who would go on to become a key figure in one of the Second World War's most daring and significant operations. In 1936, Travis graduated from Poly High with a commendable record of academic and extracurricular achievements, setting the stage for his future endeavors.

After high school, Travis continued his education at Riverside Junior College, where he pursued an Associate of Arts degree, graduating in 1938. His time at the college was marked by a burgeoning interest in aviation, a field that was rapidly advancing and capturing the imagination of many young men of his generation. The late 1930s were a period of global tension and uncertainty, with conflicts brewing in Europe and Asia. Like many young Americans, Travis felt a strong call to serve his country. His growing fascination with aviation provided the perfect outlet for this patriotic impulse, combining his love for flying with a sense of duty.

In November 1938, Travis Hoover took a significant step towards his future career by enlisting in the California National Guard. This decision marked the beginning of his long and distinguished military career. Although his time in the National Guard was brief, it provided him with crucial early experience and a taste of the military discipline and structure that would define his future servicc. It was during this time that Travis began to seriously consider a career in aviation within the military.

Determined to pursue his passion for flying, Travis enrolled in the Ryan School of Aeronautics in San Diego, California, in early 1940. The Ryan School was renowned for its rigorous training programs and its ability to produce highly skilled pilots ready for the demands of military service. For Travis, this was an opportunity to transform his love of flying into a professional career. The training was intense and demanding, but it was also exhilarating. He thrived in this environment, quickly mastering the technical aspects of flying and developing the confidence that would serve him well in the challenging years ahead.

Upon completing his initial flight training at the Ryan School of Aeronautics, Travis continued his aviation education at Randolph Field in Texas. Often referred to as the "West Point of the Air," Randolph Field was one of the premier training grounds for military aviators in the United States. Here, Travis earned his wings, officially becoming a qualified pilot in the U.S. Army Air Corps. This achievement marked a significant milestone in his life, symbolizing not just the culmination of years of hard work and dedication, but also the beginning of his active service as a military officer.

Travis's journey did not stop at Randolph Field. He continued his advanced training at Kelly Field, another major military aviation base in Texas. Known for its rigorous training programs, Kelly Field was crucial in preparing pilots for the harsh realities of aerial combat. Travis's performance during this period further solidified his reputation as a highly skilled aviator. His instructors and peers quickly recognized him as a pilot with exceptional abilities, not only in technical proficiency but also in maintaining composure under pressure, a quality that would be vital in the years to come.

On 26 May 1940, Travis was commissioned as a lieutenant in the U.S. Army Air Corps. This commission marked the formal start of his military career, which would soon lead him to participate in one of the Second World War's most daring and historic missions. Following his commissioning, Lieutenant Hoover was assigned to the 17th Bombardment Group, a unit of the United States Army Air Corps. This group was among the first to receive the new B-25 Mitchell bombers, medium twin-engine aircraft that would later become famous for their role in the Doolittle Raid.

The 17th Bombardment Group was tasked with developing new tactics for using the B-25 in combat. This period was one of intense experimentation and innovation, as the Army Air Corps sought to maximize the effectiveness of this new aircraft. Travis quickly distinguished himself as an exceptionally skilled pilot within the group. His abilities did not go unnoticed, and he was soon selected for the top-secret mission which would later be known as the Doolittle Raid.

In preparation for the raid, Travis and other members of the 17th Bombardment Group underwent specialized training designed to prepare them for the unprecedented challenge of launching B-25 bombers from an aircraft carrier. As already discussed, this feat had never been attempted before and required not only advanced flying skills but also extraordinary courage. The training took place at Eglin Field in Florida under the direction of Lieutenant Colonel James H. Doolittle.

The mission was shrouded in secrecy, and the details were not fully disclosed to the volunteers until they were already at sea aboard the USS *Hornet*. Travis, driven by a deep sense of duty and a desire to strike back at the enemy, was one of the volunteers who stepped forward for this dangerous mission. He was selected as one of the twenty-four five-man crews to operate the requisitioned B-25 Mitchell bombers. The training was intense, focusing on short takeoffs, low-altitude flying, and precise bombing techniques – skills that would be critical for the success of the raid.

On 18 April 1942, after weeks of preparation, Travis piloted the second B-25 bomber during the Doolittle Raid on Tokyo. The plane to took off from the USS *Hornet* at 8:25 am on 18 April 1942, identified by its USAAF serial number 40-2292 and NAA manufacturer's serial number 62B-2961. The plane did not have a designated name.

The takeoff from the *Hornet* was particularly challenging for his plane, as rough seas caused water to wash over the bow of the carrier. The aircraft was momentarily thrown into the air, creating a precarious situation. However, through skilled piloting and remaining calm under pressure, Travis managed to stabilize the aircraft and proceed with the mission.

Travis's B-25, like the others, successfully bombed its targets. However, the mission did not end there. After completing their bombing runs, the aircraft faced a long and perilous journey towards China, where they hoped to land safely. Unfortunately, Travis's B-25 ran out of fuel as they neared the Chinese coast, leading to a forced wheels-up crash landing in a muddy rice paddy near the town of Zhuangqiao, China, which is located in the vicinity of Ningbo, Zhejiang Province. Despite the challenging conditions, Travis's exceptional piloting skills ensured that all five crew members survived the crash.

After the crash landing, Travis and his crew found themselves in enemy-occupied territory. Realizing the importance of preventing the Japanese from capturing any valuable information, equipment, or technology from the downed aircraft, Travis and his crew set the plane on fire using a gas-soaked tarpaulin. This quick thinking ensured that nothing of strategic value fell into enemy hands. The next three days were a tense and dangerous ordeal as the crew evaded Japanese patrols, relying on their instincts and the support of local Chinese guerrillas who helped guide them through the treacherous terrain.

Their journey took a fortunate turn when they met Tung Sheng Lin, a courageous Chinese student fluent in English and familiar with the local terrain. Lin risked his life to guide the crew to safety, playing a crucial role in preventing their capture by Japanese forces. His efforts, along with those of other Chinese resistance fighters, were instrumental in the successful evacuation of several Doolittle Raiders. On 14 May 1942, Travis and his crew finally reached Chongqing, the wartime capital of China. Tung Sheng Lin's actions highlighted the broader cooperation between Chinese forces and the Allies during the war and underscored the vital role local support played in the success of the Doolittle Raid.

Following his participation in the Doolittle Raid, Travis continued to distinguish himself in combat operations throughout the remainder of the Second World War. He flew numerous missions across various theaters, including North Africa and Italy, piloting a range of aircraft such as B-25 Mitchell bombers, B-24 Liberator bombers, and P-38 Lightning fighters. His contributions were marked not only by his bravery and skill as a pilot but also by his leadership and ability to adapt to rapidly changing combat environments. For his valor and dedication, Travis earned several commendations and awards.

After the war, Travis transitioned to peacetime life and married Coella Fern “Kay” Vorhies on 21 December 1947, in Miami, Oklahoma. Through this union, he became a stepfather to Kay’s daughter, Beverly. The marriage marked a new chapter in his life, as he moved from being a wartime hero to embracing the roles of husband and father. Despite the transition to civilian life, Travis’s commitment to service remained unwavering. He continued to serve in the U.S. Air Force, playing a significant role in the development and training of new pilots and airmen.

Travis’s military service extended beyond the Second World War into the Korean War, where he commanded the 6351st Fighter Wing at Naha Air Base in Okinawa, Japan. His leadership was crucial during this conflict, as he managed air operations and ensured the readiness and effectiveness of his unit. After the Korean War, Travis continued to advance his military education and leadership skills by attending the Air University at Maxwell Air Force Base in Alabama. This period of study prepared him for even higher command responsibilities, and he played a key role in shaping military strategy and operations during the early years of the Cold War.

In February 1956, Travis took command of the 3500th Pilot Training Group at Reese Air Force Base in Texas. In this capacity, he oversaw the training of new pilots, ensuring they were prepared for the demanding nature of military aviation. His efforts were instrumental in shaping the training programs that produced the next generation of U.S. Air Force pilots. In July 1959, he was appointed deputy commander of the 3500th Pilot Training Wing, where his leadership and experience continued to be invaluable in the development of young pilots.

Travis's career continued to advance as he was appointed deputy commander of the 3610th Navigator Training Wing at Harlingen Air Force Base in Texas in September 1959. Here, he was responsible for overseeing the training of Air Force navigators, further contributing to the readiness and capability of the U.S. military. His strategic acumen and dedication to excellence in training were further demonstrated when he was assigned as the commander of the 7216th Air Base Group at Incirlik Air Base in Turkey in November 1961. This assignment was particularly significant, given Incirlik's strategic importance during the Cold War. Travis's leadership at Incirlik was vital in maintaining the operational readiness of U.S. forces in a region marked by geopolitical tension.

After completing his assignment in Turkey, Travis returned to the United States in June 1963, where he served as director of several directorates under the deputy chief of staff for technical training at Headquarters Air Training Command. His roles included overseeing the Resources and Requirements Directorate, the Training Standards and Evaluation Directorate, and the Electronic Systems Training Directorate. In these capacities, Travis played a crucial role in shaping the training and operational standards of the Air Force, ensuring that the service maintained its edge in technical proficiency and strategic readiness.

Colonel Travis Hoover's final military assignment was as commander of the 3380th Technical Training Squadron at Keesler Air Force Base in Mississippi, a role he assumed in May 1966. Keesler Air Force Base was known as a premier center for technical training, particularly in the fields of electronics and communications, which were becoming increasingly vital to military operations during the Cold War. As commander, Travis was responsible for overseeing the training of thousands of airmen in these critical disciplines, ensuring that they were not only technically proficient but also capable of adapting to the rapidly evolving technological landscape.

Under Travis's leadership, the 3380th Technical Training Squadron focused on delivering cutting-edge education that emphasized both theoretical knowledge and practical application. His approach to training was holistic, recognizing the importance of fostering a disciplined, well-rounded force capable of responding to the diverse challenges posed by a complex global environment. He was particularly noted for his ability to integrate new technologies and teaching methods into the training programs, reflecting his forward-thinking mindset and understanding of the needs of a modern Air Force.

During his tenure, Travis implemented several innovative training initiatives designed to improve efficiency and effectiveness. He was a strong advocate for using simulation and hands-on training techniques, which allowed trainees to gain practical experience in a controlled environment before they were deployed. This emphasis on experiential learning helped bridge the gap between theoretical knowledge and real-world application, better preparing airmen for the challenges they would face in their assignments around the world.

Travis also placed a high priority on developing leadership skills among the trainees. He believed that every airman, regardless of rank, had the potential to be a leader in their own right. To this end, he introduced leadership development programs that were integrated into the technical curriculum, ensuring that graduates of the 3380th were not only experts in their technical fields but also equipped with the decision-making and leadership skills necessary to succeed in high-pressure situations.

Beyond his direct responsibilities as commander, Travis played a key role in the broader strategic planning efforts at Keesler Air Force Base. He was involved in several high-level committees that aimed to align the training programs at Keesler with the overall strategic objectives of the U.S. Air Force. His insights, drawn from years of combat and command experience, were invaluable in shaping policies and training programs that would enhance the operational readiness of the Air Force.

Travis's leadership at Keesler Air Force Base was characterized by a relentless commitment to excellence. He set high standards for both his instructors and trainees, believing that only through rigorous training and discipline could the U.S. Air Force maintain its technological edge and strategic superiority. His ability to inspire those around him was evident in the high morale and strong performance of his squadron. Many of the airmen who trained under his command went on to have distinguished careers, attributing their success to the foundations they built at Keesler under Travis's mentorship.

Travis's final years of service were marked by his efforts to ensure that the Air Force's training programs remained relevant in the face of rapid technological changes and shifting geopolitical landscapes. He was acutely aware of the challenges posed by the Cold War, particularly the need for a technically skilled and highly adaptable force capable of responding to a wide range of threats. His forward-thinking approach to training helped prepare the Air Force to meet these challenges, leaving a lasting impact that extended well beyond his tenure.

On 31 October 1969, Colonel Travis Hoover retired from the United States Air Force after more than three decades of distinguished service. His retirement marked the end of a remarkable career that had spanned the prelude to the Second World War, the war itself, the Korean War, and much of the Cold War. Throughout this period, Travis had made significant contributions to both combat operations and the training and development of Air Force personnel. His commitment to excellence, his leadership in times of both conflict and peace, and his unwavering dedication to service were hallmarks of his career.

Upon retirement, Travis received numerous accolades from his peers and superiors, recognizing his exceptional service and contributions to the Air Force. He was celebrated not only for his tactical acumen and bravery in combat but also for his strategic vision and innovative approach to training and leadership development. The respect he commanded from those who served with him was a testament to his integrity, professionalism, and the high standards he set throughout his career. Travis's legacy at Keesler Air Force Base and within the broader Air Force training community is enduring.

Even after his retirement, Travis's influence was felt within the Air Force community. He remained a respected figure, often called upon for his insights and advice on matters related to training and leadership. His life after retirement was marked by continued engagement with the military community, where he shared his experiences and wisdom with the next generation of military leaders. His contributions to the field of military aviation and training are remembered as a crucial part of the Air Force's development during a pivotal period in its history.

Travis Hoover took care of his mother for the last eight years of her life, demonstrating his close relationship with her. Elizabeth lived to be over 100 years old. Sadly, Travis passed away on 17 January 2004, in Joplin, Missouri, after nearly a year of declining health and a recent battle with pneumonia. He was 86 years old at the time of his death. Colonel Hoover had been widowed since 1990, when his beloved wife Kay passed away. He left behind a stepdaughter, five grandchildren, and seven great-grandchildren, as well as a legacy of bravery, dedication, and service.

Travis was laid to rest at Fort Sam Houston National Cemetery in San Antonio, Texas, where he joined the ranks of other distinguished military veterans. As the last surviving member of his Doolittle Raid crew, his passing marked the end of an era. His life and career are remembered not only for his participation in that raid, but also for his continued service to his country during both wartime and peacetime.

Colonel Travis Hoover's legacy is one of courage, leadership, and unwavering commitment to his country. His contributions to the United States Air Force and his role in one of the Second World War's most audacious missions have secured his place in history as a true American hero. His story continues to inspire generations of servicemen and women who follow in his footsteps, dedicating their lives to the defense of freedom and the pursuit of peace. Travis's life is a testament to the values of hard work, perseverance, and patriotism that he learned in his youth and carried with him throughout his distinguished career.

Travis's journey from a small town in New Mexico to the skies over Tokyo and beyond is a testament to the enduring spirit of the American serviceman – a spirit that continues to inspire and guide the U.S. military to this day.

Pilot of Crew 3

Captain Robert M. Gray

Captain Robert Manning "Bob" Gray was born on 24 May 1919, in the small, close-knit community of Elijah, Texas. This rural town, nestled in the heart of Texas, was a place where the rhythms of life were dictated by the land and the seasons. The people of Elijah shared a strong sense of community, where neighbors were more than just those who lived nearby, they were friends, family, and confidants, united by common experiences and mutual support. The deep-rooted traditional values of this region, where hard work and integrity were paramount, played a significant role in shaping Robert's character from a young age. His parents, Cordelia "Della" Manning and James Marvin Gray, were hard-working individuals who believed in the virtues of diligence, education, and service to others. These principles, instilled in Robert and his older sister, Marjorie, would guide Captain Robert M. Gray throughout his life, from his early years in Texas to his final days as a decorated military aviator.

Growing up in Elijah, Robert experienced a childhood that, while simple, was rich in the values that would later define his life. The rural setting provided him with ample opportunities to develop a deep connection with the natural world around him. The community in Elijah was self-sufficient, relying on the land for sustenance and livelihood. This environment fostered a sense of self-reliance and responsibility that was evident in Robert's daily activities. The Gray family, like many in the area, lived off the land, and young Robert quickly became accustomed to the hard work that came with rural life. From a young age, Robert was involved in the daily chores that kept the family going. He learned to milk cows, tend to livestock, and help with the planting and harvesting of crops. These tasks were not just a part of daily life; they were essential for the family's survival and instilled in Robert a strong work ethic that would carry him through the challenges he would face later in life.

The values of hard work, integrity, and perseverance were not just taught, but demonstrated by Robert's parents. His father, James, was a man of strong principles who believed that success was earned through dedication and effort. He taught Robert the importance of honesty and the value of a day's work. His mother, Cordelia, was equally influential in shaping Robert's character. She instilled in him a love for learning and a deep sense of compassion for others. She believed that education was the key to a better life and encouraged Robert to pursue his studies with diligence. These values, imparted by his parents, laid the foundation for the man Robert would become.

When Robert was still a young boy, the Gray family made a pivotal move to Killeen, Texas. This relocation marked a significant turning point in Robert's life. At that time, Killeen was a burgeoning town in Bell County. Before Camp Hood, later Fort Hood, was established in 1942, the area around Killeen was primarily rural and sparsely populated, with a landscape dominated by ranches, farmland, and small communities. The town of Killeen itself was founded in 1882 as a railroad town, named after Frank P. Killeen, an assistant general manager of the Gulf, Colorado and Santa Fe Railway. The arrival of the railway spurred some growth, but Killeen remained a modest agricultural center in the early twentieth century.

In Killeen, the Gray family settled on Tenth Street, close to the Quality Hardware store on 6th Street, which was owned and operated by Robert's father, James. The store was more than just a business – it was a vital part of the community, serving as a gathering place for locals and providing essential goods and services. Through his involvement in the family business, Robert developed a strong sense of responsibility and learned the value of contributing to the local economy. This early experience in the family business not only helped Robert understand the importance of hard work but also introduced him to the principles of leadership and service.

The move to Killeen also opened up new opportunities for him. The town was larger and more developed than Elijah, with better schools and more resources. Robert quickly adapted to his new surroundings and became active in both his community and school. He attended Killeen Elementary School and later Killeen High School, where he began to distinguish himself academically and athletically. The educational system in Killeen was still developing, but it was a place where young minds were nurtured, and Robert quickly emerged as a standout student. His teachers recognized his potential and encouraged him to pursue his interests in science and engineering.

As a child, Robert was not only active in his community but also involved in agricultural activities, which were a staple of life in rural Texas. He participated in raising sheep and cattle for local agricultural shows, a tradition that connected him with the land and taught him important lessons about hard work, discipline, and perseverance. He learned that success was not achieved overnight but through consistent effort and determination.

Robert's love for the outdoors extended beyond his daily chores. One of his favorite pastimes during his youth was riding his pinto pony, Whiskey Pete. The bond between boy and horse was strong, and Whiskey Pete became a symbol of Robert's adventurous spirit. This passion for adventure and exploration would later translate into his affinity for flying, sparking a determination to become a pilot, a dream that would soon lead him to the skies.

At Killeen High School, Robert continued to excel both in the classroom and on the athletic field. He was a member of the high school football team, where his speed and agility earned him the nickname "Bullet Bob." As a receiver, Robert was known for his quickness on the field, a trait that mirrored his sharp intellect and keen decision-making skills in the classroom. His leadership qualities were evident early on, as he was respected by his peers and teachers alike. His success in high school laid the groundwork for his future endeavors, as he developed a strong sense of teamwork and leadership. These qualities would prove invaluable as he transitioned from a small-town boy to a military aviator during one of the most challenging periods in history.

Upon graduating from Killeen High School in 1936, Robert's journey led him to John Tarleton Agricultural College in Stephenville, Texas. This institution, which would later become part of the Texas A&M University system, was known for its demanding academic programs and its emphasis on agricultural and technical education. At Tarleton, Robert immersed himself in his studies and continued to cultivate his interests in engineering and mechanics. He excelled academically, and his time at Tarleton solidified his desire to further his education in a field that combined his technical skills with his love for aviation.

After two years at Tarleton, Robert made the pivotal decision to transfer to Texas A&M University, one of the premier engineering schools in the nation. At Texas A&M, Robert majored in aeronautical engineering, a decision that would set the course for the rest of his life. The rigorous curriculum at Texas A&M,

coupled with the institution's emphasis on discipline, service, and leadership, provided Robert with the tools he needed to succeed in the rapidly evolving field of aviation. His studies at Texas A&M were not just about academic achievement; they were about preparing for a life of service and innovation in a world that was on the brink of war. The academic environment at Texas A&M was challenging, but it was also a place where Robert's leadership abilities began to shine. He became involved in various student organizations and continued to develop the skills that would later make him a successful military leader.

The move to Texas A&M also provided Robert with the opportunity to interact with other students who shared his passion for aviation and engineering. He was able to learn from experienced professors and gain hands-on experience with the latest technology in the field. This exposure to cutting-edge advancements in aviation further fueled his desire to become a pilot. Robert's dedication to his studies paid off, and he graduated with honors in 1940, earning a degree in aeronautical engineering. This achievement marked the beginning of his journey toward becoming a military aviator.

Robert graduated with the Class of 1940, earning his degree in aeronautical engineering and cementing his path toward becoming an aviator. Although his graduation marked the culmination of years of hard work and dedication, it was also just the beginning of a journey that would take him from the classrooms of Texas A&M to the skies over war-torn Asia.

As the Second World War loomed on the horizon, like many young men of his generation, Robert felt a strong call to serve his country. The attack on Pearl Harbor on 7 December 1941 had galvanized the nation, and Robert was determined to do his part in the defense of the United States. Shortly after graduating from Texas A&M, he enlisted as a flying cadet in the United States

Army Air Corps on 24 June 1940, in Dallas, Texas. The Flying Cadet Program was a challenging training initiative designed to transform cadets into skilled military pilots capable of meeting the challenges of wartime aviation. It was a path that required both physical endurance and mental acuity, qualities that Robert possessed in abundance.

The training program was designed to push cadets to their limits, both physically and mentally, as they learned the intricacies of military aviation, including classroom instruction on aerodynamics and aircraft systems, and hands-on flight training. Robert's background in aeronautical engineering gave him a significant advantage in understanding the complexities of aircraft mechanics and aerodynamics, which made him a standout among his peers. His technical expertise, combined with his unwavering dedication to his training, quickly earned him a reputation as one of the most promising cadets in his class.

Training also included rigorous physical conditioning, so Robert's days were filled with early morning drills, followed by hours of classroom lectures and flight simulations. The cadets were taught to fly in a variety of conditions, including night flying, instrument flying, and formation flying. They also received instruction on navigation, weather, and aircraft maintenance. The training was designed to prepare the cadets for the challenges they would face as military pilots, including the ability to remain calm under pressure and make split-second decisions in the air.

On 8 February 1941, Robert achieved a major milestone in his military career when he received his pilot wings and was commissioned as a lieutenant in the United States Army Air Corps. The ceremony took place at Kelly Field, near San Antonio, Texas, one of the primary training bases for military aviators at the time. This day marked Robert's official entry into the ranks of military pilots.

Following his commissioning, Lieutenant Gray's first assignment was with the 34th and later the 95th Bombardment Squadron of the 17th Bombardment Group. Stationed at McChord Field in Washington State, Robert was trained to fly the B-25 Mitchell bomber, an aircraft that would become synonymous with the Doolittle Raid. The B-25 was a versatile and powerful aircraft, capable of delivering a significant payload over long distances. It was well-suited to the type of mission that Robert and his fellow aviators would soon undertake. The 17th Bombardment Group was one of the first units to be equipped with the B-25, and the experience Robert gained during this time was instrumental in his selection for a pivotal role in the war effort.

By early 1942, Lieutenant Gray had proven himself as an exceptional pilot. His skills, combined with his dedication and leadership, led to his selection as a volunteer for the top-secret mission that became known as the Doolittle Raid, a bold and risky operation designed to strike a retaliatory blow against Japan following the attack on Pearl Harbor.

In preparation for the raid, Robert and other members of the 17th Bombardment Group underwent specialized training at Eglin Field, Florida. The training was grueling, pushing the men to their physical and mental limits. The risks were high, but Lieutenant Gray and his fellow raiders were driven by a deep sense of duty and patriotism. They knew that the success of the mission would depend on their ability to perform under the most challenging conditions.

The details of the mission were revealed to the raiders aboard the USS *Hornet* after departing from San Francisco on 2 April 1942. The mission was fraught with danger, as the bombers would be flying at the extreme limit of their range, with little margin for error. As discussed earlier, as the task force neared Japan the convoy was spotted by Japanese picket boats, forcing the mission to be launched earlier than planned. This development added an additional layer of complexity and risk to an already perilous operation.

At 8:30 am on 18 April 1942, Lieutenant Robert M. Gray piloted the third B-25 bomber to take off from the USS *Hornet* during the raid on Tokyo. His plane, which he named after his beloved pony Whiskey Pete, was tasked with bombing the industrial area in the Shiba Ward of Tokyo. The B-25 bomber bore the USAAF serial number 40-2270 and NAA manufacturer's serial number 62B-2939.

The raid succeeded in its primary objective, demonstrating that Japan was vulnerable to American air attacks and boosting Allied morale. The success of the raid sent shockwaves through Japan, shaking the confidence of the Japanese military.

After successfully completing their bombing run, Robert and his crew faced the daunting task of reaching safety in China. Due to fuel shortages, they were forced to bail out over Quzhou, in Zhejiang Province, China, an area perilously close to Japanese-occupied territory. The bail out marked Robert's first parachute jump, a harrowing experience that saw him and his crew landing in unfamiliar terrain under cover of darkness. The jump was fraught with danger, as the crew members were scattered across a remote and hostile landscape, with no guarantee of rescue.

The Chinese people in the region played a crucial role in rescuing and sheltering the crew members, helping them evade Japanese capture. The Chinese resistance fighters and civilians who aided the American airmen did so at great personal risk, as the Japanese military was known for its brutal reprisals against those who assisted Allied forces. Despite the dangers, the Chinese people showed incredible courage and generosity, ensuring that Robert and his crew were eventually able to make their way to safety. The relationships formed during this time highlighted the global nature of the conflict and the shared humanity that transcended borders and cultures.

The escape from Japanese-occupied China was a perilous journey. The crew members had to navigate through rugged terrain, avoid Japanese patrols, and find food and shelter in a land where they were strangers. The Chinese people who helped them were often poor farmers or villagers who risked their lives to protect the American airmen. The bonds of friendship and gratitude that were formed during this time would have a lasting impact on the survivors.

Unfortunately, the raid was not without its losses. Corporal Leland D. Faktor, one of Robert's crew members, was killed during the bail out. Some accounts suggest that Faktor may have remained with the plane and was found deceased in the wreckage. His death was a tragic reminder of the risks involved in the mission and the sacrifices made by those who served. Despite the loss, the remaining crew, including Robert, managed to evade capture and were eventually escorted to safety by Chinese resistance fighters and civilians.

Following the Doolittle Raid, Robert remained in the China-Burma-India theater, where he continued to serve as a B-25 pilot with the 11th Bomb Squadron of the 7th and later 341st Bomb Group. He participated in several critical missions in the region, contributing to the Allied war effort in one of the most challenging theaters of the war. The China-Burma-India theater was characterized by its harsh terrain, extreme weather conditions, and the constant threat of Japanese attacks. Despite these challenges, Robert continued to serve with distinction, demonstrating the same bravery and dedication that had marked his participation in the Doolittle Raid.

The CBI theater was often referred to as the "forgotten theater" of the Second World War because it received less attention than the European and Pacific theaters. However, the challenges faced by the men who served there were no less daunting. The terrain was among the most difficult in the world, with high mountains, dense jungles, and treacherous rivers. The weather was unpredictable, with monsoons, heat, and humidity making life miserable for the troops. The Japanese forces in the region were well-entrenched, and the Allies had to fight for every inch of ground.

Robert's missions in the CBI theater were crucial to the success of the Allied war effort. He flew bombing raids against Japanese supply lines, transportation hubs, and military installations, helping to disrupt the enemy's operations and weaken their ability to wage war. These missions were often conducted under extremely hazardous conditions, with limited resources and support. Despite the dangers, Gray remained committed to his duty and continued to serve with distinction.

On 18 October 1942, the war effort in the China-Burma-India, CBI theater was reaching a critical juncture. The Japanese forces had established a strong presence in the region, and the Allied forces were under immense pressure to disrupt their operations. Among the brave men tasked with these high-risk missions was Lieutenant Richard Joyce, a seasoned pilot who had earlier taken part in the Doolittle Raid as pilot of Crew 10. On this day, however, fate took a different turn.

Lieutenant Joyce was at the field hospital in Dinjan, India, recovering from an illness or injury that rendered him unable to fly. Despite his condition, the urgency of the mission could not be overstated. The target was a Japanese convoy near Hong Kong, a strategic objective that, if successfully attacked, could significantly hamper Japanese supply lines and military operations in the region.

With Joyce grounded the mission needed a replacement pilot, someone with experience, courage, and a willingness to face the high stakes involved. Robert, already a distinguished pilot in the CBI theater, volunteered to take Joyce's place. Gray's decision to step into the role was a testament to his dedication and bravery, knowing full well the dangers that lay ahead.

Joining Gray on this mission was a handpicked crew:

- Co-pilot Max F. West: An experienced aviator whose skills complemented Gray's own.
- Bombardier co-pilot Richard A. Walter: Responsible for the precision bombing required to hit the Japanese convoy.
- Gunner Herbert F. Cromwell: Tasked with defending the bomber from enemy fighters.
- Gunner George E. Larkin: A veteran of the Doolittle Raid, where he had served as a gunner in pilot Joyce's Crew 10.
- Private Russell D. Juggers: A passenger on this flight, who, like the rest of the crew, shared the risks of the operation.

The crew's collective experience and camaraderie were crucial for the mission's success, but the dangers they faced were equally formidable. Shortly after taking off from Dinjan, Robert and his crew set course for their target. The mission demanded that they fly over some of the most inhospitable terrain in the world, skirting the towering peaks of the Himalayas and navigating through unpredictable weather patterns that could change from clear skies to severe storms in minutes. The low-altitude approach needed to bomb the convoy increased the risk of encountering mechanical issues, as the aircraft would be operating at the limits of its capabilities.

About thirty minutes into the flight, disaster struck. Both engines of the B-25 Mitchell bomber failed simultaneously, a catastrophic mechanical failure that left the aircraft with no thrust, no lift, and no possibility of maintaining altitude. The crew's training and experience would have kicked in immediately as they tried to troubleshoot the issue, but with both engines out, their options were severely limited.

At such a low altitude, there was little time to react. The dense jungles and rugged mountains offered no safe landing sites, and the bomber, now powerless, was at the mercy of gravity. The plane plummeted towards the earth, and the inevitable crash that followed was devastating. The impact was so severe that all aboard, Robert, co-pilot Max F. West, bombardier co-pilot Richard A. Walter, gunners Herbert F. Cromwell and George E. Larkin, and passenger Private Russell D. Juggers, were killed instantly.

The loss of Lieutenant Gray and his crew sent shockwaves through their unit and the broader Allied forces in the CBI theater. The men who had volunteered for the mission were not just seasoned professionals; they were brothers-in-arms, united by the shared hardships and dangers of war. Their deaths were a stark reminder of the perils faced by those who served in this often overlooked theater of operations.

The news of the crash quickly spread through the ranks. Efforts to locate and recover the remains of the crew were launched, but the challenging terrain made this a difficult and dangerous task. The retrieval teams, driven by a sense of duty and respect for their fallen comrades, navigated through treacherous conditions to reach the crash site. Eventually, they were successful in recovering the bodies of Robert and his crew, ensuring that these brave men would be honored and remembered for their sacrifice.

The bodies of Robert Gray, George Larkin, and the rest of the crew were transported to Barrackpore, a British air base located north of Calcutta (Kolkata) in India. Barrackpore was a key military installation during the war, serving as a logistical hub and a place where many wounded soldiers were treated. It was also home to the 7th Bomb Group, making it a fitting location for the final resting place of these airmen.

The decision to bury the crew at Barrackpore was not just a matter of logistics, it was a symbolic act of respect and honor. The base had seen many airmen pass through its gates, some of whom, like Robert and his crew, would not return from their missions. The burial at Barrackpore served as a solemn reminder of the cost of war and the personal sacrifices made by those who served in far-flung corners of the globe.

Today, the memory of Captain Robert M. Gray and his crew endures as a powerful testament to the courage and dedication of those who served in the China-Burma-India theater. Their story is a poignant reminder of the dangers faced by Allied airmen and the ultimate price paid by many in the fight against tyranny. The bravery of these men, who volunteered for some of the most dangerous missions of the war, continues to inspire and resonate with those who learn of their sacrifice.

The CBI theater may have been the "forgotten theater," but the heroism of men like Robert ensures that it will never be forgotten. Their legacy lives on in the annals of history, in the memories of their families, and in the hearts of those who continue to honor the sacrifices made in the name of freedom.

The loss of Major Robert Manning Gray, George Larkin, and their crew on 18 October 1942, is a poignant example of the countless untold stories of bravery and sacrifice that occurred in the CBI theater. Their mission, like many others, was part of the broader Allied strategy to disrupt Japanese supply lines and maintain pressure on Japanese forces throughout Asia. These missions were critical to the overall success of the Allied war effort, yet they were often conducted under conditions that were as dangerous as any faced in the European or Pacific theaters.

The story of Robert and his crew also highlights the broader challenges of operating in the CBI theater. The region's difficult terrain, severe weather conditions, and the constant threat of enemy action made every mission a test of endurance and skill. Aircrews like Robert's were tasked with flying over some of the highest mountains in the world, often in aircraft that were pushed to their limits by the extreme conditions. Despite these challenges, the men who served in the CBI theater demonstrated remarkable resilience and determination. Their efforts contributed significantly to the eventual defeat of Japan.

The legacy of Robert Gray, George Larkin, and their crew lives on not only in the historical records but also in the memory of those who served alongside them. Their story is a reminder of the courage and dedication of all those who served in the Second World War, particularly in the often-overlooked CBI theater. It serves as a testament to the human spirit and the willingness to make the ultimate sacrifice in the pursuit of a just and necessary cause.

Captain Robert M. Gray's legacy was further honored in 1948 when a new flying facility constructed near Killeen to handle heavy bombers and support nearby military installations was named Robert Gray Air Force Base. In 1963, the base was transferred to the Army and renamed Robert Gray Army Airfield, a name it still bears today. The airfield continues to play a vital role in supporting military operations, ensuring that Robert's legacy lives on through the ongoing defense of the nation.

In addition to the airfield, Robert's memory is preserved through several other tributes. A bronze statue of Captain Robert M. Gray in his flight gear stands in the Killeen-Fort Hood Regional Airport, serving as a lasting symbol of his bravery and dedication, and an inspiration to all who pass through the airport. Online, the Veterans of Foreign Wars VFW Bob Gray Post 9192 also honors his legacy, as does his induction into the Texas Aviation Hall of Fame on 9 November 2001.

A notable story from Robert's time as a pilot recounts his final flight over Killeen. As he flew back to the West Coast after completing his training in Florida for the Doolittle Raid, Robert decided to make a low pass over his hometown. Flying so low with his B-25 that construction workers on the ground reportedly dove for cover, Robert buzzed the town's main street and the high school. The editor of the *Killeen Herald* remarked that it could be no one other than "Bob Gray." This final salute to his hometown was the last time anyone in Killeen saw him alive, and it remains a cherished memory for those who witnessed it.

Captain Robert M. Gray's legacy extends beyond his military service; it is woven into the fabric of his hometown and the nation he served. His story is not just one of bravery and sacrifice, but also of a deep connection to the community that shaped him. Killeen, Texas, remembers Robert Gray as a hometown hero, a young man who grew up with the values of hard work, dedication, and service to others, and who went on to make the ultimate sacrifice for his country. On 18 April each year, the community celebrates Captain Robert M. Gray Day, a day set aside to remember his heroic actions during the Doolittle Raid and his ultimate sacrifice in service to his country. The annual observance serves as a reminder of the impact that one individual can have on the course of history and the importance of honoring those who have given their lives in service to the nation. Robert's father, James Marvin Gray, who served as the mayor of Killeen from 1947 to 1949, passed away on 16 September 1966.

The legacy of Captain Robert M. Gray also serves as a powerful reminder of the enduring impact of individual actions in the broader context of history. His decision to enlist, his dedication to his training, and his willingness to take on the dangers of the Doolittle Raid all reflect a commitment to something greater than himself. It is a legacy that continues to resonate, not just in the monuments and memorials that bear his name, but in the stories told and retold by those who remember him.

Today, as we look back on the life of Robert Gray, we are reminded of the extraordinary courage and determination that defined the Greatest Generation. His story, like those of so many others who served during the Second World War, is a testament to the strength of the human spirit in the face of adversity. It is a story that encourages us to honor their memory by living up to the values they fought to protect.

Captain Robert M. Gray's remains were returned to the United States in February 1951 and reburied with full military honors at Killeen City Cemetery in Killeen, Texas.

Pilot of Crew 4

Brigadier General Everett W. Holstrom

Brigadier General Everett Wayne "Brick" Holstrom was born on 4 May 1916, in Cottage Grove, Oregon, a town known for its community spirit and the rugged beauty of the Pacific Northwest. His upbringing in Cottage Grove, a small town where neighbors looked out for each other and children enjoyed the freedom of roaming the surrounding fields and forests, instilled in him a deep sense patriotism and love for the outdoors. His father, John Holstrom, was a local businessman, and his mother, Neva Merle Kirk, focused on raising the family, teaching Everett and his siblings the importance of hard work, integrity, and resilience.

During his formative years, Everett likely attended one of the local elementary schools. Growing up in a modest household, young Everett developed a strong work ethic and a sense of responsibility that would guide him throughout his life. Cottage Grove's close-knit environment and the communal spirit of the town left a lasting impression on Everett, shaping his character and his future path.

Everett's journey into aviation began during the 1930s while attending Pleasant Hill High School, located in the neighboring town of Pleasant Hill. This period was transformative for him, as he developed a fascination with aviation. Witnessing early aircraft flying overhead sparked a passion that would shape the course of his life. The 1930s were a pivotal time in aviation history, marked by rapid technological advancements that captivated many young Americans. Everett was no exception, finding inspiration in the era's achievements and dreaming of becoming a pilot. The allure of flight, combined with the burgeoning possibilities that aviation represented, fueled his aspirations throughout his teenage years.

Everett earned the nickname "Brick" because of his distinctive red hair and rugged demeanor, a moniker that would stay with him throughout his life.

Beyond his passion for aviation, he was a standout figure in his high school community, known for his athleticism and leadership on the football field. His physical prowess earned him the respect of his peers, while his sense of fairness and integrity set him apart as a natural leader. These traits would later define his approach to leadership both in and out of the cockpit.

After graduating from Pleasant Hill High School in 1934, Everett embarked on a dual path of service and education. That same year, he enlisted in the Oregon Army National Guard, where he trained as a radio operator. His time in the National Guard introduced him to military life and provided him with valuable technical skills, laying the groundwork for his future career. Simultaneously, he enrolled at Oregon State College (now Oregon State University), where he majored in forestry. The college experience in the 1930s was one of intellectual growth and innovation. Everett immersed himself in his studies, preparing for the challenges ahead while keeping a keen eye on the evolving world of aviation.

The atmosphere at Oregon State College was charged with the excitement of new ideas and technologies, particularly in the fields of aviation and engineering. Everett, who had long been drawn to the skies, found himself inspired by the advancements happening both at home and abroad. This period of intellectual exploration solidified his desire to pursue a career in aviation, and his experiences at Oregon State College provided him with a broader perspective on the technological and engineering challenges of the time.

As the 1930s progressed, so did Everett's aspirations. In December 1939, as global tensions mounted and the world edged closer to conflict, he enlisted in the Aviation Cadet Program of the U.S. Army Air Corps at Fort Lewis, Washington. This was a decisive step in his journey toward becoming a pilot. Around the same time, the U.S. government launched the Civilian Pilot Training Program, a nationwide initiative designed to increase the number of qualified pilots as the possibility of war loomed. The program aimed to prepare young Americans for roles in the aviation sector, both for civilian and military purposes. Everett seized this opportunity to hone his flying skills, seeing it as the next logical step in his pursuit of a career in aviation.

Everett quickly distinguished himself in the U.S. Army Air Corps, where his natural talent for flying became apparent. His instructors noted his ability to quickly grasp the intricacies of aircraft mechanics and his skill in mastering complex flight maneuvers. Everett's attention to detail, quick reflexes, and ability to remain calm under pressure earned him high praise from his superiors. These qualities would prove invaluable in his later career as a military aviator, where split-second decisions and composure in the face of danger were often the difference between life and death.

His time in the U.S. Army Air Corps not only provided him with practical skills, but also cemented his reputation as a capable and reliable pilot. The technical challenges of aviation, combined with the physical and mental demands of military training, were a perfect fit for Everett's strengths. He approached his training with a determination to excel, seeing it as his chance to turn his lifelong passion into a profession.

Everett's path from a small high school in Pleasant Hill to the skies as an Army Air Corps cadet was shaped by the spirit of innovation and ambition that defined the 1930s. With each step, from high school to college, from the National Guard to the Air Corps, Everett's passion for aviation deepened. His leadership skills, honed on the football field and in his studies, would serve him well as he prepared to take on greater responsibilities as a pilot. The experiences of these formative years set the stage for what would become an illustrious career in aviation, where his love of flying and his natural leadership abilities would elevate him to new heights.

As the world edged closer to war, Everett felt a call to serve his country. In December 1939, he enlisted in the U.S. Army Air Corps at Fort Lewis, Washington, a significant step that marked the beginning of a remarkable military career. Fort Lewis was a major training ground for U.S. Army personnel, and it was here that Everett began to hone his skills as a future military leader.

Everett's initial flight training took place at Kelly Field, Texas, one of the primary flight training facilities for the U.S. Army Air Corps and renowned for its rigorous training program and ability to produce some of the world's finest aviators. Everett excelled in his training, displaying a natural aptitude for flying and a keen understanding of aviation tactics. He graduated in 1940 and was commissioned as a lieutenant on 30 August of that year.

His first major assignment was with the 95th Bomb Squadron, a unit tasked with coastal defense and anti-submarine patrols, a crucial role as the threat of war loomed ever closer to American shores. Everett's commitment to his duties and his quick adaptability to the demands of military life set him apart early in his career.

Everett married Harriet "Hattie" Holstrom, (née Fisher) in Pierce, Washington on 30 August 1941. The couple had five children.

When the attack on Pearl Harbor on 7 December 1941 thrust the United States into the Second World War, the need for capable and courageous military personnel became more urgent than ever. On 24 December 1941, Everett's squadron reportedly destroyed what was believed to be the first enemy submarine off the West Coast of the United States. This event was significant in the immediate aftermath of Pearl Harbor, as fears of further attacks gripped the nation. However, there has been debate among historians regarding the accuracy of this claim, with some suggesting that the crew may have mistakenly bombed a whale instead. Despite this uncertainty, the mission underscored the challenges faced by military personnel during the chaotic early days of the war.

In the wake of Pearl Harbor, Everett was among those who stepped forward, driven by a sense of duty and a desire to contribute to a decisive American response. Everett and his crew were selected as one of the twenty-four five-man crews to operate the B-25 Mitchell bombers for the Doolittle Raid. Like the others, he trained at Eglin Field, Florida, under the supervision of Lieutenant Colonel Doolittle.

On 2 April 1942, the USS *Hornet*, carrying the chosen sixteen B-25 bombers and their crews, departed from San Francisco under a veil of secrecy. The Doolittle Raiders, as they came to be known, faced incredible challenges during their journey across the Pacific. The mission was fraught with risks from the outset, including the potential for early detection by Japanese patrols, the dangers of taking off from a moving carrier, and the limited fuel capacity of the bombers.

Everett's plane was unnamed and bore the USAAF serial number 40-2282 and NAA manufacturer's serial number 62B-2951. It was the fourth to take off from the USS *Hornet* on 18 April 1942 at 8:33 am, and encountered immediate difficulties. Shortly after takeoff, Corporal Bert M. Jordan, the engineer-gunner, reported that the turret gun was not functioning, leaving the bomber vulnerable with only a single .30-caliber nose gun for defense. As they approached the Japanese mainland, Everett's crew came under attack from four Japanese fighters. With limited defensive capabilities and low on fuel, Everett made the strategic decision to jettison the bombs into Tokyo Bay and Sagami Bay, rather than risk a direct confrontation. This decision likely saved his crew from certain destruction.

Despite this setback, Everett and his crew continued their flight toward China, aiming for safety in the designated landing zones. However, due to the early launch of the raid and the subsequent fuel shortages, they were unable to reach these zones. Forced to bail out over the city of Shangrao in Jiangxi Province, China, Everett and his crew began a grueling journey to evade Japanese patrols. With the aid of Chinese guerrillas, they managed to evade capture and were eventually brought to safety in Chongqing after several days of hiding and moving through hostile territory.

On 30 April 1942, Everett and other surviving members of the raid were honored by Madame Chiang Kai-shek in Chongqing. This recognition was a powerful symbol of the cooperation and mutual respect between American and Chinese forces during a critical period of the war.

After the raid, Everett continued to serve with distinction in the China-Burma-India theater. He was assigned to the 11th Bomb Squadron of the 341st Bomb Group, where he flew numerous B-25 missions targeting Japanese supply lines and bases from April 1942 to January 1943. These missions were vital to the Allied efforts in the region, disrupting Japanese logistics and weakening their ability to sustain their campaigns. Everett's leadership and bravery were evident throughout his service, earning him a promotion to commander of the 11th Bomb Squadron.

Everett's tenure as commander was marked by numerous successful operations against Japanese forces. His experience from the Doolittle Raid and his understanding of aerial tactics proved invaluable. Under his command, the squadron conducted effective bombing runs and provided crucial support to ground forces, further solidifying his reputation as a skilled and courageous leader.

In June 1943, after a successful tour in the China-Burma-India theater, Everett returned to the United States. He and Hattie traveled together selling U.S. war bonds, and they decided that "Brick" would make the Air Force his career. Hattie had her hands full, keeping and moving the household frequently, while caring for an expanding family – five children were born between 1942 and 1949. Everett also took on various stateside assignments, including training new pilots and developing innovative tactics for the expanding air war. His work in these roles was instrumental in preparing the next generation of aviators and refining the Air Corps' combat strategies.

Following the Second World War, Everett continued his service during the Cold War, a period marked by rising tensions between the United States and the Soviet Union. From October 1946 to April 1947, Everett was deployed to Alaska, where he played a key role in the defense of America's northern frontier. Alaska's strategic location made it a critical outpost for monitoring and countering potential Soviet threats, and Everett's work helped establish its importance in U.S. military strategy.

Everett's career progressed with a series of high-profile assignments. He served as the chief of the combat operations branch with Headquarters Strategic Air Command, first at Andrews AFB, Maryland, and later at Offutt AFB, Nebraska, from May 1948 to May 1950. These roles placed him at the heart of America's strategic planning during the early years of the Cold War, as the U.S. military developed new doctrines and capabilities to counter the Soviet threat. His expertise in aviation and strategy was critical in shaping the development of new tactics and technologies that would define the Air Force's role in global security.

In the 1950s, Everett's focus shifted to strategic reconnaissance, a field that was becoming increasingly important as the Cold War intensified. He served in various leadership positions, including as director of operations and training with the 91st Strategic

Reconnaissance Group and later the 91st Strategic Reconnaissance Wing. These assignments were crucial in maintaining the operational readiness of America's reconnaissance aircraft, which played a vital role in gathering intelligence on Soviet activities. His contributions during this period were pivotal in the development and refinement of U.S. Air Force strategies and capabilities. His leadership was instrumental in ensuring that American Air Forces were prepared to respond to any threat, maintaining a high level of readiness and effectiveness throughout his tenure.

Everett's career continued to advance with a series of command positions. From June 1955 to April 1957, he commanded the 301st Bomb Wing at Barksdale AFB, Louisiana, leading the wing to new levels of operational excellence. Under his leadership, the 301st Bomb Wing earned recognition for its performance in strategic bombing exercises, demonstrating its capabilities as a key component of America's strategic bomber force.

Following his command of the 301st Bomb Wing, Everett served as deputy commander of the 4th Air Division and later as chief of the operations plans division with Headquarters Strategic Air Command at Offutt AFB from June 1957 to September 1959. These roles placed him at the center of America's strategic planning efforts during a time of heightened tensions with the Soviet Union. Everett's work in developing and refining operational plans helped ensure that the Strategic Air Command was prepared to execute its mission in the event of a conflict.

Everett's final command positions included leading the 4130th Strategic Wing at Bergstrom AFB, Texas, and later the 43rd Bomb Wing at Carswell AFB, Texas. His leadership during these assignments was marked by the successful execution of numerous training exercises and operational missions, further demonstrating his ability to inspire and lead his men effectively.

Everett concluded his distinguished military career as the United States deputy chief of staff for the secret planning group LIVE

OAK with NATO at Mons, Belgium, from September 1966 until his retirement on 1 July 1969. In this critical role, he played a key part in coordinating the defense strategies of NATO member nations during a period of significant geopolitical tensions. His contributions to LIVE OAK were vital in ensuring that NATO remained a unified and effective force in the face of potential threats from the Warsaw Pact.

Upon retiring from the Air Force in 1969, Brigadier General Everett W. Holstrom and his wife Hattie, decided to embark on a new adventure that would mark the beginning of a fresh chapter in their lives. Having spent decades dedicated to military service and traveling across the globe, they were ready to settle into a more peaceful and stable environment. To celebrate this new phase, Everett decided to purchase a new car in New Jersey, a reliable and comfortable model well-suited for the kind of journey he had in mind.

The decision to buy a car wasn't just practical, it was symbolic. After years of flying high above the earth in various military aircraft, Everett now wanted to explore the country at ground level, to reconnect with the land he had served so faithfully from the skies. With their new car packed and ready, Everett and Hattie set out on a cross-country drive, a journey that would take them from the bustling East Coast to the serene landscapes of Monterey County, California.

The trip across America was more than just a physical journey; it was a chance for the couple to reflect on their past and look forward to their future. They took their time, enjoying the freedom of the open road. Along the way, they marveled at the diversity of the American landscape, from the rolling Appalachian Mountains to the vast Great Plains and the majestic Rocky Mountains. Each stop along their route was an opportunity to meet new people, explore small towns, and appreciate the simple pleasures of traveling together.

As they neared the West Coast, their journey brought them to the picturesque Carmel Valley, a lush area known for its scenic beauty, mild climate, and close-knit community spirit. Here, they unexpectedly crossed paths with the owners of Carmel Valley Manor, a well-regarded retirement community nestled among the valley's hills. The meeting seemed almost serendipitous. Over a casual conversation, the owners learned of Everett's extensive background in leadership and management, honed over decades of military service.

The owners, impressed by Everett's demeanor and the wealth of experience he carried with him, saw a unique opportunity. They were looking for someone who could manage Carmel Valley Manor with the same dedication, integrity, and sense of duty that Everett had shown throughout his military career. They believed he was the perfect candidate to lead the retirement community into a new era, ensuring that residents received the highest level of care and attention.

Everett, intrigued by the offer and recognizing the chance to apply his skills in a new, meaningful way, accepted the position. He and Harriet decided to settle in Carmel Valley, enchanted by its tranquil beauty and the warm welcome they received from the community. Everett quickly embraced his new role as manager of Carmel Valley Manor, where he would serve from 1969 until 1983. His leadership and management experience proved invaluable; he brought a disciplined yet compassionate approach to his work, focusing on the wellbeing and comfort of the residents.

Under Everett's leadership, Carmel Valley Manor thrived. He implemented new operational strategies to improve the community's services, ensuring that each resident felt cared for and valued. His attention to detail, combined with a deep empathy for the needs of older adults, created a supportive and nurturing environment. Everett was known for his open-door policy, often seen walking the grounds, engaging with residents, and listening to their concerns. His presence was both reassuring and inspiring, and he quickly became a beloved figure in the community.

Meanwhile, Hattie continued her long-standing commitment to service. She became actively involved in the community, drawing on her experiences as an Air Force wife to provide comfort and support to the residents and their families. She organized social events, volunteered with local organizations, and became a familiar face at the Manor, where her kindness and empathy endeared her to all who knew her.

Together, Everett and Hattie spent their retirement years surrounded by the beauty of Carmel Valley, contributing to the community that had welcomed them with open arms. Their cross-country journey had brought them to a place where they could continue their lifelong commitment to service, albeit in a different capacity. Their time at Carmel Valley Manor was marked by warmth, compassion, and a continued dedication to making a positive difference in the lives of others.

Everett's tenure at Carmel Valley Manor lasted until 1983, when he decided to retire fully. His legacy there was one of integrity, leadership, and unwavering commitment to the well-being of the residents. He and Hattie continued to enjoy their life in Carmel Valley, surrounded by their children, grandchildren, and great-grandchildren. The journey they had begun so many years ago in a new car from New Jersey had led them to a community they would come to call home, a place where they could continue to live out the values of service, dedication, and love that had defined their lives together.

Brigadier General Everett W. Holstrom passed away on 2 December 2000, in Carmel Valley, California. He died from a brain hemorrhage at the age of 84. Following his death, he was honored with a full military funeral and was laid to rest with full military honors at Arlington National Cemetery in Arlington, Virginia, reflecting his distinguished service and dedication to his country.

Everett's death marked the end of a life dedicated to service, both to his country and to the people he encountered along the way. He was cremated, and his ashes were interred at Arlington National Cemetery in Arlington, Virginia, a fitting resting place for a man who had given so much to his nation.

His legacy is one of courage, leadership, and unwavering dedication to the principles of freedom and democracy. As a member of the Doolittle Raiders, he played a crucial role in a mission that demonstrated to the world that the United States would not be defeated. His contributions to the Air Force and to his country will be remembered for generations to come, a testament to the enduring spirit of those who serve.

Everett was one of five Doolittle Raiders who later became general officers, alongside James H. Doolittle, John A. Hilger, David M. Jones, and Richard A. Knobloch. His story is a reflection of the bravery, resilience, and strategic thinking that characterized the U.S. military's approach during some of the most challenging periods in modern history. Everett's life and career serve as an inspiring example of service and dedication, embodying the values of duty, honor, and country.

Pilot of Crew 5

Major General David M. Jones

Major General David Mudgett "Davy" Jones was born on 18 December 1913, in Marshfield, Oregon, into a family characterized by resilience and determination. His father, David Arthur Jones, was a civil engineer of Welsh descent whose expertise in building and design profoundly influenced young David. His mother, Grace Cameron Mudgett, played a nurturing role, instilling in him a strong sense of curiosity and a passion for learning. Growing up in Marshfield, a small but industrious coastal town known for its shipbuilding and timber industries, David was surrounded by mechanical ingenuity and the transformative power of engineering.

The city of Marshfield, Oregon, officially changed its name to Coos Bay in 1944. The change was made to better reflect its geographical location near the bay and the Coos River, and to unify the identity of the area with the adjacent body of water. The name "Coos Bay" is now used to refer to both the city and the natural bay, and it remains the largest city on the Oregon coast.

From a young age, David Jones exhibited a fascination with how things worked. He was known for taking apart household objects to study their mechanisms and for his keen interest in the machinery at work in the local industries. This curiosity was more than just a childhood phase; it laid the foundation for his lifelong passion for engineering and aviation. His early education at Marshfield

Elementary School was marked by a particular aptitude for subjects that allowed him to explore his mechanical inclinations, such as mathematics and science.

Marshfield's close-knit community provided a supportive environment that valued education and hard work. Teachers and family members quickly recognized David's potential and encouraged his academic pursuits. These early experiences not only shaped his intellectual development but also laid the groundwork for the disciplined and focused approach that would characterize his later achievements. The importance of education, coupled with a strong work ethic, was instilled in him from a young age.

David likely attended elementary school in his hometown during the early 1920s. Given his birth year and the fact that he moved to Tucson, Arizona, in the late 1920s, it is reasonable to suggest that David received his early education in Marshfield. During this period, he would have attended one of the local elementary schools, where he developed the foundational skills that would later support his distinguished career. His formative years in Marshfield would have shaped his early experiences before moving to Tucson as a teenager.

The family's move to Tucson in the late 1920s, was a move that would significantly impact David's educational trajectory. Enrolling in Tucson High School, David continued to excel academically, particularly in mathematics and science. The high school offered a more advanced curriculum than what had been available in Marshfield, allowing him to delve deeper into subjects that intrigued him. His analytical mind thrived in this environment, and he quickly became known for his strong performance in technical subjects.

During his high school years, David also engaged in various extracurricular activities, where he honed his leadership skills and learned the value of teamwork. These experiences outside the classroom were just as formative as his academic achievements, helping him develop a character that would serve him well in his future. Despite his academic success, David's interests were not confined to the classroom. He was fascinated by aviation, a field that was rapidly evolving during his youth. The advancements in flight technology and the exploits of early aviators captured his imagination. This passion for flight would eventually steer him away from a conventional engineering career and toward a life in the military.

After graduating from Tucson High School in the early 1930s, David pursued higher education at the University of Arizona, where he enrolled in the mining engineering program. He graduated in 1932 with a degree in mining engineering, having distinguished himself as a diligent and capable student. Mining engineering was a field that offered a challenging and intellectually stimulating environment, well-suited to David' talents. The University of Arizona's engineering program was renowned for its rigor, and he thrived in this demanding academic setting.

David's time at the University of Arizona was more than just an academic endeavor; it was a period of personal growth and exploration. He further developed his problem-solving abilities, learning to approach complex challenges with a methodical and analytical mindset. These skills would later prove invaluable in his military career, particularly in situations that required quick thinking and decisive action. Moreover, his college years solidified his interest in aviation. The university's engineering curriculum provided him with a deep understanding of mechanical systems, which complemented his growing interest in aircraft and flight.

During his time at university David joined the Arizona National Guard and was initiated into the Sigma Chi fraternity. The Arizona National Guard is a branch of the United States National Guard, serving as a state militia with both federal and state missions. It consists of the Arizona Army National Guard and the Arizona Air National Guard. Members of the Arizona National Guard can be called upon to serve in times of national emergency or during state-level crises, such as natural disasters or civil disturbances.

While primarily under the control of the state governor, the Arizona National Guard can also be mobilized by the federal government to support active-duty military operations. Members often serve part-time while also pursuing civilian careers or education, making it a vital component of both local and national defense efforts.

The Sigma Chi fraternity is one of the largest and oldest collegiate fraternities in North America, founded in 1855 at Miami University in Ohio. It is a social fraternity focused on fostering lifelong friendships, leadership development, and academic achievement among its members. It emphasizes values such as integrity, mutual respect, and brotherhood, encouraging its members to live by a strong set of ethical standards.

Upon earning his degree, David initially considered a career in the mining industry, but his passion for aviation soon led him in a different direction. The 1930s were a time of great innovation in aviation, with rapid advancements in aircraft design and flight capabilities. Inspired by these developments, David decided to pursue a career in the United States Army Air Corps.

David received his commission as a second lieutenant in the cavalry division of the Arizona Army National Guard, where he completed one year of active duty. On 26 June 1937, David enlisted in the United States Army Air Corps, marking the start of what would become a distinguished military career. Determined to become a pilot, he underwent rigorous training and earned his pilot wings at Kelly Field in San Antonio, Texas, on 17 June 1938.

David married Anita Bernice Maddox on 24 June 1939, in the town of Winters, Runnels County, Texas. Anita was born on 13 February 1918, in Brush, located in Morgan County, Colorado.

David excelled during flight training, mastering the skills needed to operate a wide variety of aircraft. His engineering background gave him an advantage, allowing him to understand the mechanical systems of the planes he flew. This technical expertise, combined with his natural talent for flying, set him apart from his peers.

Upon completing his training, David was assigned to the 95th Bombardment Squadron, part of the 17th Bombardment Group, one of the first units to receive the B-25 Mitchell bomber – the versatile twin-engine medium bomber that would play a pivotal role in the coming conflict, being used for strategic bombing, ground support, and anti-shipping missions. David quickly became proficient in flying the B-25, participating in training missions that prepared his squadron for the looming war.

As tensions in Europe and the Pacific continued to rise in the late 1930s and early 1940s, the United States began to prepare for the eventuality of entering the conflict. The 17th Bombardment Group, stationed at Pendleton Field in Oregon, was on the front lines of these preparations. David and his fellow aviators underwent intense training, focusing on the tactics and skills that would be required in combat. The training was demanding, but David's dedication and skill earned him the respect of his superiors and peers alike.

In early 1942, as the United States grappled with the aftermath of thc attack on Pearl Harbor, David volunteered for a mission that would ultimately test his skills and courage to the fullest – the Doolittle Raid.

The USS *Hornet*, along with its escort ships, would transport sixteen B-25 bombers across the Pacific to a point approximately 460 miles from Japan, where the planes would take off with sufficient fuel to reach their targets in Japan and then continue on to safe landing sites in China.

David's crew, designated as Crew 5, consisted of Lieutenant Rodney R. Wilder as co-pilot, Lieutenant Eugene F. McGurl as navigator, Lieutenant Denver V. Truelove as bombardier, and Sergeant Joseph W. Manske as engineer and gunner. His plane had the USAAF serial number 40-2283 and manufacturer serial number 62B-2952. As with some of the other planes involved in the raid, David's aircraft did not have a specific nickname, but it was identified by its crew number and serial number.

As discussed previously, the *Hornet* was spotted early by a Japanese picket boat, and so the bombers had to launch from a distance of about 625 miles from Japan, 225 miles farther away than the planned 400 miles. (This account differs slightly from Jimmy Doolittle's, which has the range at 650 miles. Accounts of the exact distance vary, ranging from 625 to 650 miles, depending on the specific crew's recollections or records.) This significantly increased the challenge of the mission due to fuel limitations and the increased distance to their targets, and then on to China.

On 18 April 1942, David and his crew successfully took off from the *Hornet* at 8:37 am and bombed their assigned target in Tokyo. The takeoff was a harrowing experience, as the bombers had to gain enough speed and lift to become airborne in a very short distance. Once airborne, the bombers flew at low altitude across the Pacific, evading Japanese radar as they approached their targets. David and his crew successfully bombed their assigned target in Tokyo, causing damage to military installations and factories.

After completing their bombing run, David and his crew faced the daunting task of reaching China. The plan called for the bombers to land at airfields in China that had been secured by Chinese forces loyal to the Allied cause. As they neared the Chinese coast, it became clear that they would not have enough fuel to reach the designated airfields.

David made the difficult decision to order his crew to bail out over a mountainous region in China. The crew parachuted safely to the ground near Quzhou, but they were scattered across a remote and rugged landscape. Despite the dangers posed by Japanese patrols and the harsh terrain, the crew members were eventually reunited with the help of Chinese civilians and soldiers. The Chinese people risked their lives to shelter and guide the American airmen, leading them through treacherous conditions to safety. The journey was long and arduous, but thanks to the bravery and generosity of the Chinese people, David and his crew were able to evade capture and return to American forces. His entire crew bailed out without injury and were the first crew to arrive in Quzhou, as they landed southeast of it.

Following the success of the Doolittle Raid, David continued to serve with distinction in the United States Army Air Corps. In September 1942, he was assigned to the newly formed 319th Bombardment Group, part of the 12th Air Force. The 319th Bomb Group was deployed to North Africa as part of Operation Torch, the Allied invasion of French North Africa. David's experience and leadership were invaluable during this campaign, as the 319th Bomb Group conducted numerous bombing missions against Axis forces in Tunisia, Algeria, and Libya.

On 4 December 1942, while flying a mission over Tunisia, David's aircraft was hit by enemy anti-aircraft fire. The damage was severe, and David was forced to crash-land the plane in enemy territory. He and his crew were quickly captured by German forces and taken as prisoners of war. David was transported to a series of POW camps in Germany, eventually ending up at Stalag Luft III, a high-security camp specifically designed to hold captured Allied airmen.

Stalag Luft III, located in Sagan (now Żagań, Poland), was infamous for its stringent security measures, which included elevated huts to prevent tunneling and extensive surveillance. Despite these precautions, the prisoners at Stalag Luft III were determined to escape. David, with his background in engineering and his leadership experience, became an integral part of the escape committee, a group of prisoners responsible for planning and executing escape attempts.

The most famous of these attempts was the "Great Escape," a meticulously planned operation that involved the construction of three tunnels, code-named "Tom," "Dick," and "Harry." The escape plan was ambitious, involving extensive preparations that included forging documents, making civilian clothes, and acquiring maps and compasses. David played a key role in the planning and execution of the escape, contributing his engineering expertise to the construction of the tunnels.

The Great Escape took place on the night of 24/25 March 1944. Seventy-six men managed to crawl through the "Harry" tunnel to freedom, but the escape was ultimately compromised when the seventy-seventh man was spotted by a German guard. Of the seventy-six who escaped, only three successfully made it to neutral territories and eventually returned to Allied forces. Tragically, fifty of the escapees were recaptured and executed on orders from Adolf Hitler, in a brutal act of retaliation meant to deter future escape attempts.

Although David was not among the escapees on the night of the Great Escape, his involvement in the planning and support of the operation exemplified his courage, ingenuity, and determination. His time in Stalag Luft III was marked by numerous other escape attempts and acts of resistance against his captors. Despite the harsh conditions and the constant threat of punishment, David remained steadfast in his commitment to his fellow prisoners and to the Allied cause.

David's experiences as a POW had a profound impact on him, deepening his resolve to continue serving his country and contributing to the war effort. He remained a prisoner of war until April 1945, when he was liberated by advancing Allied forces. Upon his return to the United States, he was hailed as a hero for his bravery during the Doolittle Raid and his resilience during his time in captivity.

After his liberation and return to the United States, David resumed his military career, continuing to serve with distinction in a variety of leadership roles. In the immediate aftermath of the Second World War, he was assigned as an air inspector at Headquarters

Air Training Command, where he played a key role in shaping the post-war training programs for the newly established United States Air Force.

In 1946, David attended the Armed Forces Staff College, where he further developed his strategic and leadership skills. This training prepared him for the increasingly complex challenges he would face in the post-war world, as the United States emerged as a global superpower and the Cold War began to take shape. David's experience and expertise made him a valuable asset to the Air Force, and he was soon entrusted with a series of high-profile assignments.

One of his first major post-war assignments was as director of war plans at Headquarters Tactical Air Command. In this role, David was responsible for developing and implementing strategic plans for the Air Force's tactical operations. His work during this period was instrumental in shaping the Air Force's approach to air combat and ground support, ensuring that the United States remained at the forefront of military aviation.

David's expertise in bombing tactics and his experience from the Doolittle Raid made him a natural choice to lead the development of new bombing techniques. As director of combat operations at 9th Air Force, he oversaw the testing and implementation of these techniques, which included the use of low-level bombing and precision strikes. These innovations would prove crucial in the Air Force's operations during the Korean War and beyond.

In February 1952, David was appointed commander of the 47th Bomb Wing at Langley AFB, Virginia. Under his leadership, the 47th Bomb Wing became one of the Air Force's most capable and effective units, known for its high operational readiness and innovative tactics. In June of that year, David was transferred to RAF Sculthorpe in England, where he continued to command the 47th Bomb Wing until June 1955. During this time, he played a key role in strengthening the United States' air capabilities in Europe, working closely with NATO allies to ensure the security of Western Europe during the early years of the Cold War.

David's contributions to military aviation were not limited to tactical operations. In April 1958, he was appointed deputy chief of staff for operations at the Air Proving Ground Command at Eglin AFB, Florida. In this role, he oversaw the testing and evaluation of new aircraft and weapons' systems, ensuring that the Air Force remained at the cutting edge of technological innovation. His work during this period was critical to the development of the B-58 Hustler, the world's first operational supersonic bomber.

In August 1960, David was appointed commander of the 6592nd Test Squadron, where he directed the B-58 Hustler Test Force at Carswell AFB, Texas. The B-58 Hustler was a groundbreaking aircraft, capable of flying at speeds in excess of Mach 2 and carrying a nuclear payload. David's leadership was instrumental in the successful development and deployment of this aircraft, which became a key component of the United States' nuclear deterrent during the Cold War.

David's contributions to aviation extended beyond the Air Force. In August 1964, Major General David M. Jones was appointed deputy chief of staff for systems with Headquarters Air Force Systems Command at Andrews AFB, Maryland. In this role, he was responsible for overseeing the integration and development of complex systems that were critical to the Air Force's operational capabilities. His work during this period helped to ensure that the Air Force remained at the forefront of technological innovation.

In December 1964, David embarked on a new and exciting chapter in his career when he was appointed deputy associate administrator for manned space flights with NASA. This role placed him at the forefront of the United States' efforts to win the space race against the Soviet Union. The 1960s were a time of intense competition between the two superpowers, and the stakes were high. The success of the Apollo program, which aimed to land a man on the moon and return him safely to Earth, was seen as a crucial measure of American technological and scientific prowess.

David's experience in aviation, engineering, and leadership made him an ideal fit for this role. He was tasked with overseeing the planning and execution of key missions within the Apollo program, working closely with some of the nation's top scientists and engineers. His contributions to the space program were significant, helping to ensure that NASA met its ambitious goals.

One of Major General Jones's key responsibilities was to ensure the safety and reliability of the spacecraft and systems used in the Apollo missions. This required meticulous attention to detail and an understanding of the complex technologies involved. David's engineering background and his experience in military aviation provided him with the expertise needed to address the numerous challenges that arose during the development of the Apollo program.

During his time at NASA, David was involved in several critical missions, including the early Apollo flights that tested the capabilities of the spacecraft and systems. These missions were essential in building the foundation for the successful moon landing in 1969.

In May 1967, David returned to military service as commander of the Air Force Eastern Test Range at Cape Kennedy, Florida. The Eastern Test Range was a key component of the United States' space program, serving as the launch site for many of the country's most important space missions. In this role, David was responsible for overseeing the testing and launch operations at Cape Kennedy, ensuring that the missions were conducted safely and successfully.

David's leadership at Cape Kennedy was instrumental in the success of numerous missions, including those associated with the Apollo program. His leadership and technical expertise helped to ensure that the United States remained at the forefront of space exploration, and his contributions to the space program were recognized as a key factor in the success of the Apollo missions.

After a long and distinguished career, David M. Jones retired from the United States Air Force on 1 June 1973, at the rank of major general. His retirement marked the end of a remarkable journey that had seen him rise from a young boy with a passion for mechanics to one of the most respected and accomplished leaders in the history of the U.S. Air Force.

Sadly, David's wife Anita passed away in 1993. In 1994 he relocated to Texas, settling in Air Village II, a residential community in San Antonio, Texas, which is often associated with military personnel and veterans. It provides housing for those who have served in the armed forces, offering a close-knit environment with facilities and support catering to their needs. San Antonio itself is home to several military bases, including Joint Base San Antonio, making it a significant hub for military life. After fifty years of serving retired military officers and their families, Air Force Village has expanded its eligibility to include all former military personnel, as well as seniors without a military background. As part of this transition, the two campuses in San Antonio have been renamed Blue Skies of Texas.

In January 1999 David married Janna-Neen Cunningham, the widow of his longtime friend, General Joseph Cunningham. They divided their time between their residence in Air Village, San Antonio, and their home in Tucson, Arizona.

Major General David M. Jones passed away in Tucson on 25 November 2008, at the age of 94, due to natural causes associated with old age. He was laid to rest with honors at Arlington National Cemetery in Arlington, Virginia. His legacy is one of bravery, innovation, and leadership. His remarkable career left a lasting influence on military aviation and on the space race, securing him a prominent place in American history. From his wartime service during the Second World War to his role in the Cold War and space exploration efforts, Jones's achievements continue to inspire new generations of aviators, engineers, and leaders.

General David M. Jones is remembered as one of five Doolittle Raiders who achieved the rank of general, alongside James H. "Jimmy" Doolittle, Jack A. Hilger, Everett W. Holstrom, and Richard A. Knobloch. These men embodied the courage and leadership that defined their generation.

Pilot of Crew 6

Lieutenant Dean E. Hallmark

Lieutenant Dean Edward "Jungle Jim" Hallmark was born on 20 January 1914, in the small West Texas town of Robert Lee, a place emblematic of the rugged, frontier spirit that characterized much of early twentieth-century Texas. Dean was the son of Ollie Dean Hallmark, born on 25 December 1888, in Llano, Texas, and Raleigh Amanda Ake, born on 25 December 1892, in Las Cruces, Doña Ana County, New Mexico. Dean's sister, Mozelle Amanda Hallmark, followed on 11 November 1918, in South Sulphur, Hunt County, Texas. Dean's upbringing in this environment forged his strong work ethic and resilience, traits that would later define his military career.

The Hallmark family's roots were deeply embedded in the agricultural traditions of West Texas. Dean's grandfather farmed land between Robert Lee and Bronte, focusing primarily on cotton, a demanding crop that required intense labor and an understanding of the land. The family's involvement in cotton farming, a staple of the Texas economy, was reflective of the broader agricultural landscape of the region, which was characterized by its reliance on cotton as a cash crop. This background instilled in Dean a profound respect for hard work and the cycles of nature. The family's additional connections to Hill Country, where they grew pecans, further diversified their agricultural activities, contributing to a deep-seated understanding of the land and its offerings.

Dean's father was a multifaceted worker who held various jobs throughout his life, reflecting the economic challenges and resourcefulness required in rural Texas. As a cattle buyer in Greenville, Texas, Ollie was well acquainted with the ups and downs of the livestock market, a volatile industry heavily influenced by external factors such as weather, disease, and market demand. His work as a carpenter and painter also demonstrated his adaptability and skill in different trades, further showcasing the resourcefulness needed to provide for a family in such an environment.

Dean spent much of his childhood in Greenville, Texas, a city that played a pivotal role in his early development. Located north of Dallas, Greenville was known as the cotton capital of the world during this period, with vast fields of cotton surrounding the city and contributing to its economic prosperity. The city's bustling atmosphere, fueled by the cotton industry, offered young Dean a glimpse of the broader world beyond the rural landscapes of West Texas.

Growing up in Greenville, Dean was immersed in a community where hard work and determination were valued above all else. The city's economic success was largely built on the back of its working-class citizens, who toiled in the fields, factories, and various trades to make a living. This environment of industriousness and resilience deeply influenced Dean, who from a young age worked alongside his father, contributing to the family's livelihood. These experiences not only taught him the importance of perseverance and responsibility but also fostered a sense of duty and commitment that would later become hallmarks of his character.

Dean's formal education began at Travis Elementary School in Greenville, where he was exposed to the foundational subjects of reading, writing, and arithmetic. This education was typical of the time, focusing on the basics needed to succeed in a world where manual labor was often the norm. However, the school also placed a strong emphasis on values such as discipline, respect, and duty, instilling in Dean a sense of order and purpose that would guide him throughout his life. These formative years were crucial in shaping Dean's future, as they provided him with the basic skills and mindset that would later characterize his service in the military.

After completing his elementary education, Dean continued his studies at Greenville High School, where he excelled both academically and athletically. The high school years were a time of significant growth for Dean, as he began to emerge as a leader among his peers. His natural athleticism led him to American football, where he quickly became a standout player. As a lineman for Greenville High School's football team, Dean played a key role in leading the school to its first appearance in the Texas State playoffs in 1931. This achievement was a source of great pride for both Dean and his community, highlighting his talent and determination on the field.

Football, however, was more than just a sport for Dean, it was a means of learning important life lessons. The discipline, teamwork, and perseverance required to succeed on the football field were qualities that Dean carried with him. His experiences in high school, both in the classroom and on the football field, laid the groundwork for the man he would become, a man characterized by his unwavering commitment to his goals and his readiness to face challenges head-on.

Following his success in high school, Dean's athletic abilities earned him a place at Paris Junior College in Texas, where he continued to develop his skills as a lineman. His prowess on the football field did not go unnoticed, and in 1935, he received a full football scholarship to Alabama Polytechnic University, now known as Auburn University. This opportunity was a significant achievement for Dean, as it allowed him to further his education while continuing to pursue his passion for football.

At Auburn, Dean played under the legendary coach Ralph "Shug" Jordan, who would later become one of the most respected figures in college football history. Under Jordan's guidance, Dean continued to excel on the field, showcasing his strength, agility, and strategic thinking. Standing tall and strong, with a physique honed through years of hard work on the family farm, Dean was a dominant force on the field. His physical presence and skill made him a key player for the Auburn Tigers, contributing to the team's success during his time at the university.

Although he spent a year in the 'Loveliest Village' at Auburn studying education, Dean's time at Auburn was not without its challenges. In addition to the rigorous demands of balancing academics and athletics, Dean faced personal difficulties that would ultimately alter the course of his life. His father, Ollie, was involved in a tragic accident which resulted in the loss of a leg, and this likely prompted Dean to return home to assist his family. This sense of duty to his family was a testament to the strong values instilled in him during his upbringing. Such an accident would be a debilitating blow for anybody, but Ollie's determination to continue working despite this severe disability served as a powerful example to Dean of perseverance and strength in the face of adversity.

In addition to the family crisis, Dean suffered a leg injury and aggravated a recurring hip injury that eventually required surgery. These injuries not only ended his promising football career but also marked a significant turning point in his life. On 12 January 1936, Dean underwent surgery at St Margaret's Hospital in Montgomery, Alabama, effectively bringing his time at Auburn to a close. While this marked the end of his football aspirations, it also opened the door to new opportunities and challenges that would shape the rest of his life.

After leaving Auburn, Dean's life took a new direction as he sought employment with the Humble Oil & Refining Company in Houston, Texas. As a machinist working in the oil fields of Lake Charles, Louisiana, Dean developed technical skills and a strong work ethic. The oil industry, particularly in Texas and Louisiana, was booming during this period, offering young men like Dean the chance to learn valuable trades and gain hands-on experience in a rapidly growing field. Dean's work with Humble Oil involved maintaining and repairing machinery, tasks that required precision, attention to detail, and an understanding of mechanical systems.

Around 1937, Dean joined the seismograph team of the Standard Oil Company, agreeing to be transferred to Venezuela. His work in South America, which included time spent in Dutch Guiana and Suriname, took him to remote, jungle-like areas, where he earned the nickname "Jungle Jim." This nickname, inspired by a comic strip hero who fought Japanese guerrillas in the 1930s, reflected Dean's adventurous spirit and his ability to adapt to challenging and unfamiliar environments. His experiences in the jungles of South America not only tested his physical endurance but also broadened his perspective on the world. Living and working in these remote areas required a level of resourcefulness and resilience that few possessed. These experiences helped prepare him for the rigors of military life, where adaptability and endurance would prove crucial.

In 1940, Dean returned to Texas with a new goal in mind: to become a pilot. His decision to pursue aviation was driven by a desire to serve his country, a sense of adventure, and a fascination with the burgeoning field of aviation. The world was on the brink of war, and Dean was eager to contribute to the defense of his country in a meaningful way. Dean enrolled at the University of Texas to participate in the Civilian Pilot Training Program, where he took his first flight on his 26th birthday at Love Field in Dallas. This experience ignited a passion for aviation that would define the rest of his life. Flying offered Dean a sense of freedom and excitement that he had not experienced before, and he quickly became dedicated to mastering the skills required to become a pilot. He continued flying throughout the spring and summer, honing his skills and building his confidence as a pilot. He completed his final check ride and received his pilot's license at Stinson Field in San Antonio, Texas, a milestone that marked the beginning of his journey into military aviation. This accomplishment was a testament to Dean's determination and hard work, as he had successfully transitioned from a career in athletics, then oil, to one in aviation.

On 21 November 1940, Dean Hallmark enlisted in the Aviation Cadet Program of the U.S. Army Air Corps in Houston, Texas. The Aviation Cadet Program was designed to rapidly train and commission officers who would serve as pilots, navigators, and bombardiers – roles that were crucial as the United States prepared for the possibility of entering the global conflict.

After completing basic training in Ontario, California, Dean underwent advanced training at Moffett Field and Stockton Field, both in California. These training programs were intense and demanding, designed to prepare cadets for the challenges of aerial combat. The training included both ground school, where cadets studied navigation, meteorology, and aircraft mechanics, and flight training, where they learned to operate military aircraft under various conditions. On 11 July 1941, Dean graduated from his training, earning his wings and being commissioned as an officer. Earning his wings was not just a personal triumph, it was a validation of his decision to pursue aviation and a recognition of his readiness to serve as a pilot in the U.S. Army Air Corps.

Immediately after his training, Dean was assigned to the 95th Bombardment Squadron, 17th Bombardment Group, stationed at Pendleton Field in Oregon. The unit was among the first to be equipped with the new B-25 Mitchell bomber, making Dean one of the first pilots to fly the aircraft that would later play a crucial role in the historic Doolittle Raid. The aircraft's design allowed it to perform a variety of roles, from bombing runs to reconnaissance missions, and it quickly became a favorite among pilots for its ruggedness and adaptability. Dean's assignment to fly the B-25 was a reflection of his skills as a pilot and his ability to handle one of the most advanced aircraft in the Army Air Corps' arsenal.

In early 1942, following the Japanese attack on Pearl Harbor, the United States was thrust into the Second World War. The need for skilled pilots became more urgent than ever, and Dean and his crew were ordered to fly anti-submarine patrols along the West Coast, protecting American shores from potential enemy threats. These patrols were critical in safeguarding the United States from the possibility of further attacks and in maintaining control over the vital sea lanes along the coast.

In February 1942, just days after starting his new duties in South Carolina, Dean and the rest of the 17th Bombardment Group were presented with an extraordinary opportunity. Volunteers were sought for a dangerous but unspecified mission involving the B-25 bombers. Without hesitation, Dean volunteered, joining the other brave men who would soon become known as the Doolittle Raiders.

Dean trained with the other volunteers at Eglin Field in Florida, where the crews practiced the short takeoffs, low-level flying, and bombing techniques crucial for the success of the mission.

The audacious mission to bomb Tokyo and surrounding areas was finally revealed to the volunteers on the deck of the USS *Hornet* after departing from San Francisco on 2 April 1942. Lieutenant Colonel James H. Doolittle, the mission's planner and leader, knew it was possible for the heavily loaded bombers to take off from the short deck of a Navy aircraft carrier and had prepared meticulously for the mission. However, as we now know, the task force, comprising two aircraft carriers, fourteen support ships, and two submarines, were spotted by enemy picket boats earlier than expected. These picket boats were used to alert their mother ship upon sighting enemy vessels. Fearing that the boat had sent a warning to Japan, the American convoy immediately sank both fishing boats. Faced with the possibility of an imminent enemy attack, the commanders of the convoy and the crews of the sixteen planes on the flight deck of the USS *Hornet* were forced to make a critical decision: either take off immediately or risk being pushed overboard to make room for naval fighters needed to defend the fleet. The decision was made to take off earlier than planned, despite the risks involved.

Lieutenant Dean Hallmark was designated as the pilot of the sixth plane to take off from the *Hornet*. On 18 April 1942, at 8:40 am, Dean took off in the "Green Hornet," USAAF serial number 40-2298 and NAA manufacturer number 62B-2967, with his crew. The sixteen well-trained pilots set course for Tokyo, Yokohama, Nagoya and Kobe with the primary objective being industrial sites. After successfully bombing targets in downtown Tokyo, Dean and his co-pilot, Lieutenant Robert J. Meder, followed the course set by their navigator, Lieutenant Chase J. Nielsen, towards China.

The early takeoff, however, resulted in all sixteen aircraft running low on fuel, making it impossible for them to reach their intended destinations in China. Dean's plane was forced to make an emergency landing on the water just off the Chinese coast due to the fuel shortage. The following account is based on the testimony of the only survivor of the crew, navigator Lieutenant Chase J. Nielsen.

As the "Green Hornet" neared the Chinese coastline, the crew realized they were critically low on fuel and wouldn't make it to their intended landing site. Dean, with his experience and skill, attempted an emergency water landing. However, the conditions were against them. It was twilight, and rain severely limited visibility, making a safe landing incredibly difficult. In a desperate move, Dean tried to steer the plane to reduce the impact as they touched down on the water. Unfortunately, just as he was attempting to make this emergency landing, the plane ran out of fuel and lost all power, forcing them into a crash at approximately 9:55 pm – over thirteen hours since they had taken off from the *Hornet*.

During the attempted landing, the "Green Hornet" struck the water with its left wing first. The impact was severe, causing the left wing to break off immediately upon hitting the water. This abrupt loss of structural integrity caused the plane to veer violently, destabilizing it further and compounding the chaotic and dangerous situation for the crew.

Following the crash landing of the "Green Hornet" in the East China Sea, the crew's survival efforts were hampered by multiple equipment failures. Dean was ejected from the aircraft during the crash, sustaining severe injuries to his legs. Dean ended up in the water but managed to save himself from drowning by extricating himself from the pilot seat. Lieutenant Meder and Sergeant Dieter were also catapulted through the navigation window. The crew climbed onto the sinking plane with their life jackets on. They had intended to swim to the coast together, but high waves made this impossible.

The situation became even more critical when the floating reserve boat, which was supposed to provide a lifeline in the rough waters, malfunctioned and only partially inflated. This left the crew with a barely usable flotation device in the dark, rain-soaked, and choppy seas.

In these desperate moments, only navigator Lieutenant Nielsen managed to hang onto the partially inflated boat. The rest of the crew struggled against high waves and the powerful currents, making it nearly impossible for them to stay together or find stable support. Nielsen's ability to hold onto the boat provided him with some level of buoyancy, but it offered little protection or security in the harsh conditions.

Meanwhile, the other crew members, including the severely injured Dean, were left to battle the elements with limited resources. The failure of the boat to fully inflate and support the entire crew further exemplified the dire and challenging circumstances they faced after the crash. Despite their best efforts to survive in the aftermath of the crash, the combination of equipment failure, rough seas, and physical injuries made their situation extremely perilous.

The fact that only Nielsen was able to hang onto the boat illustrates both the desperation of the moment and the tragic turn of events for the crew of the "Green Hornet," who were left to fend for themselves in treacherous cold waters far from safety.

What is also interesting to note is that just minutes before their B-25 bomber crashed into the waters of the East China Sea, pilot Lieutenant Dean Hallmark and navigator Lieutenant Nielsen discussed landing on the water. The aircraft's fuel was almost used up, so Lieutenant Hallmark, his co-pilot Lieutenant Meder and the plane's navigator Lieutenant Chase J. Nielsen, worked out a plan and selected a location. The intention was to land in the bay of present-day Hangzhou and, possibly with their inflatable lifeboat, follow one way or another the course of the river (current name is the Qiantang River) to Quzhou – the location where the raiders wanted to meet, before heading to the final meeting place in Chongqing, the capital of Free China in those days. If one looks at this on a map, the idea of landing on the water at the Hangzhou Bay was certainly possible. According to Lieutenant Chase J. Nielsen, navigator, the distance between Hangzhou Bay and their crash location was only about four minutes of flying. Unfortunately for the crew, the fuel ran out a little too early.

Two crew members, Sergeant William J. Dieter and Corporal Donald E. Fitzmaurice, drowned when the "Green Hornet" crashed. Sergeant Dieter, gunner of Crew 6 was in the nose section of the aircraft and this led to very serious injuries after the crash. Bombardier Donald E. Fitzmaurice had hit his head on something in the back of the aircraft and had a large hole in his forehead. Despite the crew's efforts, the giant waves made it impossible for them to stay together, and Sergeant Dieter and Corporal Fitzmaurice were lost in the water. Lieutenant Meder, who had been swimming with Corporal Fitzmaurice on his back, eventually lost him to the waves.

After the crash of the "Green Hornet" in the East China Sea, Lieutenants Robert Meder, Chase Nielsen, and Dean Hallmark found themselves struggling to survive. Each man battled the rough waters and strong currents as they tried to make it to shore, but their fates seemed uncertain. Exhausted and disoriented, they all arrived separately on the beach. Nielsen recalled that when he finally made it ashore, his energy completely depleted, he immediately fell asleep on the sand, his body too tired to move.

When he woke up hours later, he saw two distant shapes on the beach. Instinctively, he moved closer, realizing with a heavy heart that the bodies lying there were likely those of Sergeant William Dieter and Corporal Donald Fitzmaurice, who probably hadn't survived the crash. However, before Nielsen could get any closer to confirm his suspicions, he was discovered by a Chinese resistance fighter who had been scouting the area. Nielsen was promptly taken to a nearby guerrilla camp near Shipu, where he was reunited with Lieutenant Hallmark, and later with Lieutenant Meder. The three surviving members of Crew 6 had finally come together again, but the weight of losing their comrades was ever-present.

The Chinese guerrillas informed the Americans that they had found and hidden the bodies of Dieter and Fitzmaurice in a safe location to protect them from being discovered by the Japanese forces that were patrolling the area. The soldiers understood the importance of preserving the dignity of their fallen comrades, even in the face of such danger.

Later that afternoon, on 19 April 1942, with the assistance of the Chinese resistance fighters, Hallmark, Meder, and Nielsen returned to the beach where the bodies of their fellow crew members had been hidden from the Japanese. Sympathetic local villagers, who had been following their plight, provided two wooden coffins for the fallen men. With great care and respect, the surviving officers placed the bodies of Sergeant William Dieter and Corporal Donald Fitzmaurice into the coffins. In a solemn, secretive ceremony held under the cover of dusk, the Chinese villagers, alongside the three surviving crew members, reburied their comrades in a more secure and hidden location near Shipu Beach, ensuring the burial site would not be discovered by the Japanese occupying forces.

This quiet reburial offered a dignified and honorable resting place for Dieter and Fitzmaurice, far from the hands of their enemies. The graves, though simply marked, stood as a powerful and poignant reminder that these men had given their lives in a distant, foreign land. The compassion and respect shown by the Chinese villagers in ensuring a proper burial for the American soldiers was a profound testament to the solidarity that had formed between the Chinese people and the Allied forces during the war.

For Nielsen, Meder, and Hallmark, the reunion, though bittersweet, provided a small measure of comfort. They knew that their fallen comrades had been laid to rest with care and dignity, a final tribute to the sacrifice they had made.

After the war, Chase Nielsen returned to the location where Sergeant William Dieter and Corporal Donald Fitzmaurice had been buried. With care and reverence, Nielsen dug up the bodies of his fallen crewmates, ensuring they could be returned to the United States. Once back on American soil, Dieter and Fitzmaurice were reburied in their homeland, receiving the honors and recognition they deserved. This final act of repatriation allowed their families and comrades to honor their sacrifice properly, while the memory of the Chinese villagers' bravery and compassion in helping bury them during the war would forever be remembered as an enduring symbol of the shared humanity and mutual struggle that united people from across the world in the fight against tyranny remained an enduring symbol of international solidarity.

On 20 April 1942, the day after burying their comrades, the three surviving members of Crew 6 of the "Green Hornet" aircraft took off from the village of Shipu. Lieutenants Robert Meder, Chase Nielsen and Dean Hallmark attempted to escape to the small walled city of Wenzhou. The situation was critical; Japanese occupying forces in China were determined to find the American officers after their daring attack on Japan.

They went out to sea on board a small boat with other passengers. The wind blew in their faces and the waves crashed against the bow, while the threat of discovery loomed over them like a shadow. They knew Japanese forces were on their heels, and every shadow on the water looked like an enemy patrol boat.

Their fears soon became reality. Not long after leaving Shipu, a Japanese patrol boat emerged. The Japanese, sharp and resolute, intercepted their vessel. Tension mounted as the Japanese soldiers boarded the small boat, their eyes keenly focused on their search for the American officers.

Aware of the danger, Meder, Nielsen, and Hallmark held their breath as they hid deep within the boat. They were concealed among barrels and blankets, their bodies pressed tightly against the cold metal walls of the boat. Every movement, no matter how small, could betray them. The Japanese conducted a thorough search of the boat. They pushed goods aside, peered into dark corners, and barked harsh orders.

Yet, by some miracle, or perhaps due to the carefulness of their hiding place, the Americans were not found. Still as statues, their hearts pounding in their chests, they waited while the Japanese searched above them. What seemed like an eternity finally ended when the Japanese soldiers gave up their search. Frustrated but unsuspecting, they left the boat without finding their target.

Only when the patrol boat finally moved away did the three men dare to breathe again. They realized just how close their escape had been; luck had been on their side. This gave them just enough time to continue their journey, but they knew the danger was not yet over. The next step was to continue their journey to Wenzhou, now with the knowledge that their enemies were lurking and that every movement had to be carefully considered. The Chinese coastline remained a dangerous battlefield, where every step forward brought new risks.

The night of 20/21 April 1942, after departing from Shipu, the three surviving crew members of the "Green Hornet" spent the night in a small coastal village. Exhausted and on high alert, they stayed in a simple hut, listening intently for any sounds that might indicate the arrival of Japanese soldiers.

By the first light of 21 April they resumed their journey, determined to reach Wenzhou and the safety of its city walls. But fate struck again. Once they arrived in Wenzhou, they were hidden by Chinese guerrilla fighters who risked their lives to protect them. They thought they were safe, but the shadow of betrayal crept ever closer. Suddenly, in the afternoon of 21 April 1942, Japanese troops appeared out of nowhere, their eyes fixed on the Americans' hiding place.

Betrayal, or perhaps a simple mistake, had given them away. In a split second, the world went silent. The three men were captured and shackled. With a sense of helplessness and grim determination, they were taken away, their faces turned toward Shanghai, where an uncertain and ominous future awaited them. The Japanese occupiers now had them in their grip. In Shanghai, China they were subjected to brutal interrogations and torture by the Kempeitai, the Japanese military police. The crew's capture marked the beginning of a harrowing period of suffering and eventual execution for one of its members.

The captors were relentless, employing severe methods to extract information from the captured Americans. The men endured unimaginable pain, their bodies and spirits tested to their limits. The relentless questioning, beatings, and psychological torment left deep scars. A fate they faced with a mixture of fear and stoic resolve. The ordeal underscored the brutal realities of war and the heavy price of their daring mission.

The Bridge House Hotel in Shanghai became notorious during the Second World War as a grim center of terror, torture, and death at the hands of the Kempeitai. This once ordinary hotel was repurposed into a makeshift prison and interrogation center where countless Chinese civilians and Allied prisoners endured unimaginable horrors. Dean was among those interrogated at the Bridge House Hotel.

For further interrogation, the three American survivors were flown to Tokyo. In the Japanese capital, they were subjected to even more intense and brutal interrogations by the Japanese military authorities, who were determined to extract as much information as possible about the Doolittle Raid and other Allied military operations. The interrogations in Tokyo were harsher, involving torture and psychological pressure that pushed them to their limits. After their time in Tokyo, Dean and his fellow prisoners were flown back to Shanghai.

Meanwhile, the three survivors learned that the five crew members of Crew 16 of Pilot William G. Farrow had also been captured by the Japanese. In Shanghai, all eight were brought before a military tribunal. What followed was a mock trial, devoid of any justice. All eight captured Americans, including the members of Crew 16 and the survivors of the "Green Hornet," were sentenced to death. For five of them, the death sentence was commuted to life imprisonment. However, for the remaining three, including Dean, the sentence remained unchanged: execution. This brutal outcome confirmed their worst fears and marked the beginning of a tragic end for three of the brave Doolittle Raiders.

Lieutenants Dean E. Hallmark, William G. Farrow (Crew 16), and Sergeant Harold A. Spatz (Crew 16), were selected for execution.

On 14 October 1942, Dean was transported from the Bridge House to Kiangwan Prison.

On 15 October 1942, a black limousine arrived at Public Cemetery No. 1 near Shanghai. Lieutenant Hallmark, Lieutenant Farrow, and Sergeant Spatz were escorted out. Prison guards led them to three small wooden crosses spaced 20 feet apart. The men were forced to kneel with their backs against the crosses. Their handcuffs were removed, and their wrists were tied to the crosspieces. White cloths were wrapped around their faces, marked with a black "X" above their noses. A six-man firing squad took up positions 26 feet in front of the prisoners. At the signal, they fired their weapons. There was no need for a second volley. After the executions, the bodies were transported to the Japanese Residents Association Crematorium, where they were cremated. The ashes were placed in small boxes under false names at a local funeral home.

Lieutenant Robert J. Meder, co-pilot of Crew 6, died of malnutrition in captivity in December 1943. After the war, Captain Joseph S. Bailey, on assignment from the Department of Justice, discovered the ashes of the executed men and Meder. Lieutenant Dean Hallmark's ashes were found under the alias "J. Smith."

Back in Shipu, the graves of Sergeant Dieter and Corporal Fitzmaurice, maintained by the local villagers, stood as quiet reminders of the airmen's bravery. Though the village suffered under Japanese occupation, the memory of these men was preserved by those who had witnessed their sacrifice. The villagers' efforts to bury and honor the American soldiers reflected a deep respect and shared commitment to resisting the tyranny of the occupiers, symbolizing the broader struggle for freedom that united people across the world during the war.

Dean had written a final letter to his parents and sister before his execution, which the Japanese had promised to deliver through the International Red Cross, along with his ashes. However, this promise was not kept, and his family only learned of his death officially after the war. Dean's story is a deeply moving chapter in American history, reflecting the extraordinary bravery and ultimate sacrifice made by those who served during the Second World War.

> Dear Mother, Dad, and Sis: I hardly know what to say. They have just told me that I am liable to execution... It still seems that I am in a dream and can't believe what is happening. I wish the court would reconsider and have a heart for us and try to understand that we have people at home that love us and we them and that we would like to see them again and live in peace... Mother, you try to stand up under this and pray. And Dad, you do the same, and Sister... I don't know how to end this letter but will end by sending you all my love.

This letter serves as a testament to the courage and resilience of soldiers who faced dire circumstances during wartime. Dean's words reflect a deep yearning for life, family, and peace amid the harrowing prospect of execution.

The death of Lieutenant Dean Hallmark is a particularly somber chapter in this story. His execution, along with two other Doolittle Raiders, by the Japanese in 1942, is remembered not as an execution but as a cold-blooded murder.

Very little is known about what exactly happened between the bombing over Japan and the arrest of Crew 6. The sole survivor of Crew 6, the navigator Lieutenant Nielsen, is the only person who could provide further insights into their ordeal. To piece together this mystery, I have relied on the information shared by Nielsen about the crash in interviews, and statements in books to which he referred after the Doolittle Raid.

Lieutenant Colonel Jimmy Doolittle, mission leader and pilot of plane 1. (NARA)

Lieutenant Travis Hoover, pilot of plane 2. (NARA)

Lieutenant Robert M. Gray, pilot of plane 3. (NARA)

Lieutenant Everett W. Holstrom, pilot of plane 4. (NARA)

Captain David M. Jones, pilot of plane 5. (NARA)

Above left: Lieutenant Dean E. Hallmark, pilot of plane 6. (NARA)

Above right: Lieutenant Theodore W. Lawson Jr., pilot of plane 7. (NARA)

Captain Edward J. York, pilot of plane 8. (NARA)

Lieutenant Harold F. Watson, pilot of plane 9. (NARA)

Lieutenant Richard O. Joyce, pilot of plane 10. (NARA)

Captain Charles R. Greening, pilot of plane 11. (NARA)

Lieutenant William M. Bower, pilot of plane 12. (NARA)

Lieutenant Edgar E. McElroy, pilot of plane 13. (NARA)

Major John A. Hilger, pilot of plane 14. (NARA)

Lieutenant Donald G. Smith, pilot of plane 15. (NARA)

Lieutenant William G. Farrow, pilot of plane 16. (NARA)

The crew members of Crew 1 during the Doolittle Raid.

Pilot: Lieutenant Colonel James H. Doolittle	First row left
Co-pilot: Lieutenant Richard E. Cole	First row right
Navigator: Lieutenant Henry A. Potter	Second row left
Bombardier: Sergeant Fred A. Braemer	Second row middle
Engineer-gunner: Sergeant Paul J. Leonard	Second row right

The ranks mentioned above are the ranks held during the Doolittle Raid. (NARA)

The crew members of Crew 2 during the Doolittle Raid.

Pilot: Lieutenant Travis Hoover	First row left
Co-pilot: Lieutenant William N. Fitzhugh	First row right
Navigator: Lieutenant Carl R. Wildner	Second row left
Bombardier: Lieutenant Richard E. Miller	Second row middle
Engineer-gunner: Staff Sergeant Douglas V. Radney	Second row right

The ranks mentioned above are the ranks held during the Doolittle Raid. (NARA)

The crew members of Crew 3 during the Doolittle Raid.

Pilot: Lieutenant Robert M. Gray	First row left
Co-pilot: Lieutenant Jacob E. Manch	First row right
Navigator: Lieutenant Charles J. Ozuk	Second row left
Bombardier: Sergeant Aden E. Jones	Second row middle
Engineer-gunner: Corporal Leland D. Faktor	Second row right

The ranks mentioned above are the ranks held during the Doolittle Raid. (NARA)

The crew members of Crew 4 during the Doolittle Raid.

Navigator: Lieutenant Harry C. McCool	First row left
Pilot: Lieutenant Everett W. Holstrom	First row middle
Co-pilot: Lieutenant Lucian N. Youngblood	First row right
Engineer-gunner: Corporal Bert M. Jordan	Second row left
Bombardier: Sergeant Robert J. Stephens	Second row right

The ranks mentioned above are the ranks held during the Doolittle Raid. (NARA)

The crew members of Crew 5 during the Doolittle Raid.

Pilot: Captain David M. Jones	First row left
Co-pilot: Lieutenant Rodney R. Wilder	First row right
Navigator: Lieutenant Eugene F. McGurl	Second row left
Bombardier: Lieutenant Denver V. Truelove	Second row middle
Engineer-gunner: Sergeant Joseph W. Manske	Second row right

The ranks mentioned above are the ranks held during the Doolittle Raid. (NARA)

The crew members of Crew 6 during the Doolittle Raid.

Pilot: Lieutenant Dean E. Hallmark	First row left
Co-pilot: Lieutenant Robert J. Meder	First row right
Navigator: Lieutenant Chase J. Nielsen	Second row left
Engineer-gunner: Corporal Donald E. Fitzmaurice	Second row middle
Bombardier: Sergeant William J. Dieter	Second row right

The ranks mentioned above are the ranks held during the Doolittle Raid. (NARA)

The crew members of Crew 7 during the Doolittle Raid.

Pilot: Lieutenant Theodore W. Lawson	First row left
Co-pilot: Lieutenant Dean Davenport	First row right
Navigator: Lieutenant Charles L. McClure	Second row left
Bombardier: Lieutenant Robert S. Clever	Second row middle
Engineer-gunner: Sergeant David J. Thatcher	Second row right

The ranks mentioned above are the ranks held during the Doolittle Raid. (NARA)

The crew members of Crew 8 during the Doolittle Raid.

Pilot: Captain Edward J. York	First row left
Co-pilot: Lieutenant Robert G. Emmens	First row right
Navigator: Lieutenant Nolan A. Herndon	Second row left
Bombardier: Sergeant Theodore H. Laban	Second row middle
Engineer-gunner: Sergeant David W. Pohl	Second row right

The ranks mentioned above are the ranks held during the Doolittle Raid. (NARA)

The crew members of Crew 9 during the Doolittle Raid.

Pilot: Lieutenant Harold F. Watson — First row left
Co-pilot: Lieutenant James M. Parker Jr. — First row right
Navigator: Lieutenant Thomas C. Griffin — Second row left
Flight engineer-gunner: Technical Sergeant Edred V. Scott — Second row middle
Bombardier: Sergeant Wayne M. Bissell — Second row right

The ranks mentioned above are the ranks held during the Doolittle Raid. (NARA)

The crew members of Crew 10 during the Doolittle Raid.

Pilot: Lieutenant Richard O. Joyce — First row left
Co-pilot: Lieutenant J. Royden Stork — First row right
Navigator: Lieutenant Horace E. Crouch — Second row left
Flight engineer-gunner: Sergeant Edwin W. Horton Jr. — Second row middle
Bombardier: Sergeant George Elmer Larkin — Second row right

The ranks mentioned above are the ranks held during the Doolittle Raid. (NARA)

The crew members of Crew 11 during the Doolittle Raid.

Pilot: Captain Charles R. Greening	First row left
Co-pilot: Lieutenant Kenneth E. Reddy	First row right
Navigator: Lieutenant Frank A. Kappeler	Second row left
Engineer-gunner: Sergeant M. Jerold Gardner	Second row middle
Bombardier: Sergeant William L. Birch	Second row right

The ranks mentioned above are the ranks held during the Doolittle Raid. (NARA)

The crew members of Crew 12 during the Doolittle Raid.

Pilot: Lieutenant William M. Bower	First row left
Co-pilot: Lieutenant Thadd H. Blanton	First row right
Navigator: Lieutenant William R. Pound Jr.	Second row left
Engineer-gunner: Sergeant Omar A. Duquette	Second row middle
Bombardier: Sergeant Waldo J. Bither	Second row right

The ranks mentioned above are the ranks held during the Doolittle Raid. (NARA)

The crew members of Crew 13 during the Doolittle Raid.

Pilot: Lieutenant Edgar E. McElroy	First row left
Co-pilot: Lieutenant Richard A. Knobloch	First row right
Navigator: Lieutenant Clayton J. Campbell	Second row left
Flight engineer-gunner: Sergeant Adam R. Williams	Second row middle
Bombardier: Sergeant Robert C. Bourgeois	Second row right

The ranks mentioned above are the ranks held during the Doolittle Raid. (NARA)

The crew members of Crew 14 during the Doolittle Raid.

Pilot: Major John A. Hilger	First row left
Co-pilot: Lieutenant Jack A. Sims	First row right
Navigator-bombardier: Lieutenant James H. Macia Jr.	Second row left
Flight engineer: Staff Sergeant Jacob Eierman	Second row middle
Gunner: Staff Sergeant Edwin V. Bain	Second row right

The ranks mentioned above are the ranks held during the Doolittle Raid. (NARA)

The crew members of Crew 15 during the Doolittle Raid.

Pilot: Lieutenant Donald G. Smith	First row left
Co-pilot: Lieutenant Griffith P. Williams	First row right
Navigator: Lieutenant Howard A. Sessler	Second row left
Physician-gunner: Lieutenant Dr. Thomas R. White	Second row middle
Flight engineer: Sergeant Edward J. Saylor	Second row right

The ranks mentioned above are the ranks held during the Doolittle Raid. (NARA)

The crew members of Crew 16 during the Doolittle Raid.

Pilot: Lieutenant William G. Farrow	First row left
Co-pilot: Lieutenant Robert L. Hite	First row right
Navigator: Lieutenant George Barr	Second row left
Flight engineer-gunner: Sergeant Harold A. Spatz	Second row middle
Bombardier: Corporal Jacob D. DeShazer	Second row right

The ranks mentioned above are the ranks held during the Doolittle Raid. (NARA)

There is a quote attributed to Doolittle during his time in Chongqing a few days after the raid, which mentions two casualties – Fitzmaurice and Dieter – near Sanmen Bay in Sanmen County. This has led to speculation that they might have crashed in that area and were later washed ashore in Shipu, Shipuzhen, as mentioned by Nielsen. Given that all three members, (two drowned) of the crew came ashore separately, it is clear they were not together in a boat, adding another layer of complexity to their story. Nielsen recalled holding onto a partially deflated, leaking life raft, which indicates the dire circumstances they faced in the water.

Although the exact crash location of the "Green Hornet" is unknown today, I believe I have managed to determine the site. Using the crash data, I ran an analysis of the calculations and this enabled me to estimate the approximate location of where Crew 6 likely crash-landed in the water. I want to stress that these calculations were based solely on the data provided by Nielsen in books and interviews for newspapers and magazines. According to the results, Crew 6 crashed approximately at coordinates 29.1° N, 121.9° E. The depth at this crash location ranges from 50 to 100 meters, 164 to 328 feet. The results from these calculations align with the information received by mission leader James Doolittle, that Crew 6 went down near Sanmen Bay.

To find the crash location, you can visit my website: www.doolittle-raid.net. Click on Crews, then select Crew 6, and finally, click on Hallmark for the details on the crash location.

The exact site where Crew 6 was captured is still debated among historians. Some oral accounts suggest that the capture occurred in Shipu, while Nielsen's account places it in Wenzhou. Both perspectives are respected, but I tend to trust Nielsen's account, as it aligns more consistently when charted with all the details he provided in books and interviews about their arrest. Again, I ran an analysis based on this information and found it plausible that the crew was indeed arrested in Wenzhou.

Dean's service, marked by extraordinary courage and dedication, remains a poignant reminder of the dangers faced by pilots during the Second World War. In 1946 his ashes were taken to Hawaii and interred at Schofield Barracks, Oahu. On 17 January 1949, they were reburied with full military honors at Arlington National Cemetery in Arlington, Virginia. This final resting place, reserved for those who have served their country with distinction, is a fitting tribute to Dean's bravery and sacrifice.

Pilot of Crew 7

Major Theodore W. Lawson Jr.

Major Theodore William "Ted" Lawson Jr. was born on 7 March 1917, in Fresno, California, to Theodore William Lawson and Mayme Julia Lehnert. Growing up during this period of American history was an exciting time for Ted. As well as rapid industrialization and technological advancements, Ted was exposed to the rapidly evolving world of aviation and was fascinated by the achievements of pioneers such as the Wright brothers, and of Charles Lindbergh – whose transatlantic flight in 1927 stunned the world.

Ted's family played a significant role in shaping his character and aspirations. His father, Theodore William Lawson, worked in various trades, including carpentry and construction. He was known for his strong work ethic and sense of duty, qualities he passed on to his son. Theodore instilled in Ted a determination to succeed, no matter the obstacles. Mayme, Ted's mother, was a nurturing and supportive figure in his life. She encouraged Ted to pursue his passions and provided the emotional support that would prove essential in his future endeavors. The Lawson family was close-knit, and the values of hard work, perseverance, and responsibility were deeply ingrained in Ted from an early age.

Ted's formal education began in Fresno's public schools, where he quickly distinguished himself as a bright and inquisitive student. He had a natural aptitude for mathematics and science, subjects that fascinated him because they provided the foundational knowledge necessary to understand the mechanics of flight. Even as a young boy, Ted was captivated by airplanes. He spent countless hours reading books on aviation, building model airplanes, and dreaming of the day he would take to the skies. His interest in aviation was not merely a childhood fantasy; it was a carefully nurtured passion that he pursued with relentless dedication.

Ted Lawson likely started high school in 1931, assuming a typical four-year high school education before graduating in 1935. His time at Los Angeles High School likely provided him with the foundational education and skills that helped him succeed in his subsequent studies in aeronautical engineering at college level.

After graduating from high school in 1935, Ted likely spent 1936 preparing for his future in aviation. During this transitional year, he may have been working, saving money, or gaining practical experience in the field he was passionate about. It's possible that Ted took on a job related to aviation or pursued additional courses to broaden his knowledge, all in preparation for his next steps in education. In 1937, he took a significant step toward realizing his dream by enrolling at Los Angeles City College. At that time, the college was a vibrant institution that attracted students from diverse backgrounds, many of whom shared Ted's passion for aviation.

The college offered courses in aeronautical engineering, which provided students with the technical skills and knowledge needed to pursue careers in aviation. For Ted, this was an ideal environment to further his understanding of aircraft mechanics and engineering principles. He was a dedicated student, known for his ability to grasp complex concepts and apply them practically. Ted spent many hours in the college's laboratories and workshops, honing his skills and understanding of the intricate systems that made flight possible.

It was during his time at Los Angeles City College that Ted met Ellen Arlene Reynolds, a bright and ambitious young woman who worked as a librarian at the college. Ellen shared Ted's intellectual curiosity and drive, and the two quickly formed a deep connection. Their relationship was built on mutual respect, shared values, and a common vision for the future. Ellen admired Ted's passion for aviation and his determination to succeed, while Ted was drawn to Ellen's intelligence and the unwavering support she provided. Their relationship blossomed during their time at college, laying the foundation for a lifelong partnership that would endure the challenges of war and beyond.

In March 1940, while still a student, Ted made a pivotal decision that would change the course of his life: he joined the U.S. Army Air Corps as an aviation cadet. At the time, the U.S. Army Air Corps was actively recruiting young men with a passion for aviation, and Ted's technical background in aeronautical engineering made him an ideal candidate. He was determined to serve his country and apply his skills and knowledge in a way that would make a meaningful impact.

To support himself financially while pursuing his dream of becoming a pilot, Ted took a job in the drafting department of Douglas Aircraft Company, a leading manufacturer of military aircraft. Working nights at Douglas Aircraft provided Ted with invaluable practical experience in the aerospace industry. He was involved in projects that focused on the design and development of military aircraft, gaining firsthand experience with the cutting-edge technology and innovations that were shaping the future of aviation. This experience complemented his academic studies, giving him a comprehensive understanding of both the theoretical and practical aspects of aircraft design and operation.

Ted's military training began with basic flight instruction at Hancock Field in Santa Maria, California. The training was demanding, designed to test the cadets' physical and mental endurance. Ted excelled, quickly mastering the fundamentals of flight and demonstrating both skill and determination. After completing his basic flight instruction, Ted moved on to primary flying training at Randolph Field in Texas, known as the "West Point of the Air." Randolph Field was one of the premier training facilities for military pilots, and it was here that Ted honed his flying skills and developed the discipline required of a military aviator. The training at Randolph Field was designed to push cadets to their limits, both physically and mentally.

Following his primary training, Ted continued his education with advanced flying courses at Kelly Field, also in Texas. Kelly Field was the final stage of training for Army Air Corps pilots, where cadets learned to fly more advanced aircraft and were tested on their ability to handle the challenges of military aviation. The training at Kelly Field was grueling, with cadets spending long hours in the cockpit and undergoing rigorous evaluations. Ted's performance during this phase of his training was exemplary, and on 15 November 1940, after completing his rigorous training regimen, he was awarded his pilot's wings and was commissioned as a second lieutenant, marking the official start of his military aviation career.

Ted's first assignment after earning his wings was with the 95th Bomb Squadron, part of the 17th Bomb Group, stationed at McChord Field in Washington. McChord Field was a key military installation that played a critical role in the defense of the Pacific Northwest. Initially, Ted served as a co-pilot on B-18 Bolo medium bombers, gaining valuable flight experience and familiarizing himself with the demands of military aviation. The B-18 was a workhorse of the U.S. Army Air Corps, used primarily for patrol and reconnaissance missions. Ted's time on the B-18 allowed him to build the skills he would later need for more complex and dangerous missions.

In addition to his experience with the B-18, Ted also trained on the Douglas B-23 Dragon, an advanced medium bomber of the era. The B-23 was a significant upgrade from the B-18, featuring improved engines, better defensive armament, and greater speed. Ted's proficiency on the B-23 further demonstrated his capabilities as a pilot, and by February 1941, he had proven himself to be an exceptional aviator. As a result, he was promoted to first pilot, a significant achievement that recognized his skill and leadership potential.

Just two months later, in April 1941, Ted's unit received seven B-25 Mitchell bombers, the newest medium bombers in the Air Corps' arsenal. Ted and his unit became the first to operate this advanced aircraft, and they quickly adapted to its unique capabilities. The experience Ted gained flying the B-25 would later be crucial during the Doolittle Raid, where his skills and knowledge would be put to the ultimate test.

While stationed at McChord Field, Ted's personal life also progressed. He married Ellen Arlene Reynolds on 5 September 1941, in Coeur d'Alene, Idaho. The wedding marked a new chapter in Ted's life as he prepared to face the challenges of war. Ellen, who continued her work as a librarian, was a constant source of support, providing him with the stability and encouragement he needed during this tumultuous time. Ellen's unwavering support played a crucial role in Ted's ability to focus on his military duties, knowing that he had a strong and loving partner by his side. The couple would later have three children together: two daughters and one son.

As the United States entered the Second World War following the attack on Pearl Harbor, Ted Lawson was one of the volunteers who stepped forward to take part in this highly secretive and dangerous Doolittle Raid. Along with other volunteers, Ted formed part of twenty-four five-man crews selected to operate the requisitioned B-25 planes. However, only sixteen crews would ultimately fly the mission, with the remaining crews placed in reserve. Throughout their intensive training at Eglin Field, Florida, the mission's details were kept top secret. Only after the USS *Hornet* had set sail from

San Francisco on 2 April 1942 did the crews learn of their exact objectives – to launch an attack on Tokyo.

When the task force was spotted by Japanese picket boats earlier than expected, the commanders of the convoy feared the possibility of an imminent enemy attack. They were forced to make a critical decision: either take off immediately or risk being pushed overboard to make room for naval fighters needed to defend the fleet. The decision to take off earlier than planned added an additional layer of risk to an already dangerous mission, as the planes would now have to fly even further to reach their targets.

The decision was made to take off earlier than planned, and at 8:43 am on 18 April 1942, Ted W. Lawson piloted the seventh plane to leave the deck of the *Hornet*. His aircraft, the "Ruptured Duck," bore the USAAF serial number 40-2261 and NAA manufacturer serial number 62B-2930 and was named after a minor training accident in which its tail had scraped the ground on takeoff. The name, along with a caricature of Donald Duck with crutches, was painted on the fuselage by (a former) plane's gunner, Rodger Lovelace. The "Ruptured Duck" quickly became a symbol of the crew's determination and resilience, embodying their willingness to overcome obstacles and complete their mission.

The sixteen well-trained pilots, including Ted, successfully launched their bombers from the deck of the *Hornet* and set course for Tokyo and three other cities. The primary objective was to strike industrial sites and other strategic targets in Japan, delivering a blow to the enemy's war production capabilities. Each plane carried four bombs, and despite the challenges of navigating without landmarks, Ted and his crew successfully bombed their assigned targets before heading towards China. The success of the bombing run was a testament to the skill and determination of the Doolittle Raiders, who had overcome incredible odds to strike at the heart of the enemy. What the crews feared came true: the early takeoff from the *Hornet* left the

B-25s with insufficient fuel to reach their intended destinations in China. Instead of flying 400 miles to their target, they had to fly 625 miles. As they neared the Chinese coast, the "Ruptured Duck," began to run dangerously low on fuel.

Realizing that they would not make it to their intended landing site in Quzhou, Ted and his crew were forced to make an emergency landing on the water just off the coast of Nantian Island, near the village of Dasha. The decision to ditch the plane was a difficult one, but it was the only option left to them as they faced the very real possibility of running out of fuel over the open sea.

The crash landing was a harrowing experience. Ted attempted to bring the plane down just before the beach, but the engines failed during the descent, causing the aircraft to crash into the sea, partially on the beach. It was dusk, and the weather was rainy, adding to the difficulty of the landing. Both Ted and his co-pilot were thrown through the windscreen during the impact. Despite the severity of the crash, all five crew members survived, though most suffered serious injuries. Ted was the most injured. His face was dented, his teeth fell out, and his left leg was badly lacerated – the wound stretched from the thigh to the calf, and went deep to the bone. His left bicep was cut off, overturned in the elbow. The crew's survival was a tribute to their training and the robust construction of the B-25, which had absorbed much of the impact of the crash.

The villagers of Dasha heard the crash and quickly came to the aid of the downed crew. Despite the dangers posed by Japanese troops in the area, the villagers carried the wounded men to safety and provided them with initial care. The bravery and compassion of the Chinese villagers were instrumental in saving the lives of Ted and his crew. They risked their own lives to help the Americans, knowing that the Japanese forces would likely retaliate if they were discovered.

The next day, Chinese guerrillas from Zheng Fucheng's unit arrived and escorted the crew to the other side of the island.

Zheng Fucheng (also known as "Zheng Fufu"), along with other local Chinese civilians, played a crucial role in rescuing Ted and his crew by providing them with food, medical assistance, and eventually leading them to safety. This act of bravery and humanity by Zheng and the local population helped ensure the survival of Ted and other members of the crew, who would otherwise have been captured or killed by Japanese forces occupying China at that time. Ted later recounted these experiences in his book *Thirty Seconds Over Tokyo*, where he detailed not only the raid but also the harrowing journey to safety, aided by the courageous Chinese people like Zheng Fucheng.

From the other side of the island, they were transported by boat, sneaking past Japanese blockades, to Zhihaiyou Town in Sanmen County, and then to Linhai, where they were admitted to Linhai Hospital. The journey to Linhai was fraught with danger, as Japanese forces were actively searching for the downed crews. The guerrillas and villagers who helped Ted and his crew demonstrated extraordinary courage and resourcefulness, navigating through enemy territory to bring the Americans to safety.

Linhai Hospital, where Ted and his crew were eventually treated, was one of the few medical facilities in the region capable of handling such severe injuries. The hospital staff, despite the overwhelming demands placed on them by the war, worked tirelessly to care for the wounded crew. However, Ted's condition continued to deteriorate, and it became clear that more drastic measures were needed to save his life. His injuries were severe, and the risk of infection was high, especially in the unsanitary conditions of wartime China.

Meanwhile, Crew 15 also made a crash landing on water, not far from Crew 7's crash site. The gunner on board Crew 15's aircraft, Dr Thomas R. "Doc" White, was a trained physician. He heard from Chinese guerrilla fighters that Crew 7 had four severely wounded members, and he was determined to visit the injured crew at Linhai Hospital at all costs.

On 24 April 1942, Dr White of Crew 15, arrived at Linhai Hospital. It was then decided to transfer three of the four Crew 7 members to Enze Hospital. Ted remained in Linhai, where his condition deteriorated so severely that Dr White, with the help of local doctors, including Dr Chen Shenyan and his father, Dr Chen Xingji, had to amputate his leg. Crew members Lieutenant Dean Davenport, Lieutenant Charles L. McClure, and Lieutenant Robert S. Clever were taken to Enze Hospital where they healed from their severe injuries.

At Enze Hospital, the crew members received also treatment from Chinese doctors, who worked tirelessly to save the wounded men despite the challenging conditions. The hospital, like many medical facilities in China during the war, was operating under extremely difficult circumstances. Supplies were limited, and the medical staff was overwhelmed with casualties from the ongoing conflict. Despite these challenges, the doctors at Enze Hospital provided the best care they could, stabilizing the crew's injuries and preparing them for the next stage of their journey.

The amputation, while necessary to save Ted's life, was a devastating blow to the young pilot. The loss of his leg meant the end of his flying career, something he had worked so hard to achieve. However, Ted faced this new challenge with the same determination and resilience that had carried him through the Doolittle Raid. He knew that he was fortunate to be alive, and he was grateful to the doctors and fellow raiders who had saved his life. Despite the pain and the uncertainty of his future, Ted remained focused on recovering and returning to the United States.

Lieutenant Thomas Robert "Doc" White, Crew 15, was awarded for his actions with the Silver Star. Thanks to a risky dive into the sinking aircraft of Crew 15, Doc White managed to recover some of his medical instruments underwater and bring them ashore from the sinking plane. With these instruments, it was possible to provide appropriate treatment to Ted and others of Crew 7.

From Crew 7, flight engineer-gunner Sergeant David J. Thatcher also received the Silver Star. He rescued his four fellow Crew 7 members, including Ted, from the crashed aircraft and provided them with the best possible first aid treatment on the beach. Later, he managed to keep his four crewmates out of Japanese captivity. Thatcher was just 20 years old.

Ted's ordeal was far from over. As Japanese forces continued to advance in China, Linhai Hospital itself became a target. The news of Ted's critical condition reached Jimmy Doolittle, who was then in Chongqing, through the Chinese resistance. Knowing that Ted and Dr White were in mortal danger, a rescue plan was quickly devised. According to this plan, Lawson and White were to be taken to the city of Henyan, where a plane would pick them up and bring them to the safety of Chongqing, which was serving as China's temporary capital at the time. Edgar McElroy, pilot of Crew 13, volunteered to fly into Henyan to rescue them.

Their escape was a harrowing journey, marked by narrow escapes and the constant threat of capture. They were regularly confronted by Japanese patrols that threatened their progress; the threat of discovery loomed like a sword over their heads, and each day brought new dangers. Thanks to the determination of their Chinese guides, they made it to Henyan. Their survival depended on the bravery and determination of the Chinese people who helped them along the way. Though Henyan was safer than Linhai, the danger persisted. The Japanese Air Force bombed the city daily, with the primary target being the airstrip, the lifeline of the city. This airstrip was crucial for receiving supplies and evacuating the wounded. Every day, the runway was damaged by Japanese bombs, but every night, the local Chinese worked tirelessly to fill the craters with earth, wood, and stones. Without these efforts, the runway would have been unusable, and the evacuation of Ted and Dr White would have been impossible.

When the rescue plane finally arrived, the tension was palpable. The only lighting on the runway came from a few lanterns placed by the villagers along the edges to mark the path. In hurried circumstances, Ted and Dr White were quickly brought aboard the plane. Edgar McElroy, using the newly repaired runway, managed to take off and bring them to Chongqing, far from the advancing enemy forces.

For Ted, the Doolittle Raid was a defining moment in his life and career. Despite the severe injuries he sustained, Ted went on to write a memoir titled *Thirty Seconds Over Tokyo*, which detailed his experiences during the raid and the aftermath. The book, published in 1943, became a bestseller. Ted's writing from the hospital bed was praised for its clarity and immediacy, bringing readers into the cockpit of the "Ruptured Duck" and into the harrowing days that followed the crash. The book resonated with a nation still reeling from the attack on Pearl Harbor and searching for heroes who embodied the American spirit of resilience and determination. Ted had become one of those heroes, and his story inspired countless others to contribute to the war effort.

The impact of *Thirty Seconds Over Tokyo* extended beyond the literary world. In 1944, the book was adapted into a major motion picture of the same name, further cementing Ted's place in history. The film, which starred Spencer Tracy, Van Johnson, and Robert Mitchum, was a critical and commercial success. It brought the story of the Doolittle Raiders to a broader audience, ensuring that their courage and sacrifice would not be forgotten. The movie remains a classic of wartime cinema, continuing to inspire new generations with its portrayal of bravery and determination. The success of both the book and the film ensured that the legacy of the Doolittle Raid would endure; a reminder of the extraordinary acts of heroism that defined the Greatest Generation.

After returning to the United States and receiving extensive treatment for his injuries, Ted continued his service to his country in a new capacity. Recognizing his experience and expertise, the U.S. Army Air Forces assigned Ted to the role of liaison officer with the U.S. Air Mission to Santiago, Chile. From May 1943 to April 1944, he worked closely with Chilean military and government officials, fostering cooperation and strengthening the ties between the United States and Chile during a critical period of the Second World War. His work in this role was instrumental in maintaining and enhancing the strategic alliance between the two nations.

Despite the physical challenges he faced due to his injuries, Ted's dedication to his duties never wavered. His time in Chile not only demonstrated his resilience but also his ability to adapt to new and demanding roles. He became an ambassador of sorts for the U.S. military, using his personal experiences to build relationships and promote cooperation. His work in Chile was a testament to his commitment to the war effort, even as he faced the ongoing challenges of recovery.

However, the toll of his wartime injuries eventually led to Ted's medical retirement from the Army Air Forces on 2 February 1945. The decision to retire was not an easy one for Ted, who had dedicated his life to aviation and military service. However, the physical and emotional toll of his injuries made it necessary for him to step back and focus on his recovery and his family.

After his retirement from the military, Ted lived a relatively quiet life, but his legacy as a war hero and author endured. He continued to be honored for his service and contributions to the war effort, with *Thirty Seconds Over Tokyo*, both the book and the film adaptation, remaining a touchstone for those studying Second World War history. Ted's story is an enduring reminder of the sacrifices made by the men and women who served during the war and the lasting impact of their actions on the course of history.

Ted Lawson passed away on 19 January 1992, in Chico, California, at the age of 74. He was laid to rest with full military honors at Chico

Cemetery, in the city where he spent his final years. His legacy continues to be remembered as a symbol of bravery and innovation in military aviation history. His final resting place has become a site of pilgrimage for those who wish to pay their respects to a true American hero.

Major Ted Lawson's journey from a young man with a passion for aviation to a celebrated war hero and author is a story of perseverance, courage, and the enduring human spirit. His contributions to the Doolittle Raid and his subsequent work as an author and military liaison officer have left an indelible mark on history, ensuring that his legacy will continue to be remembered and honored for generations to come.

Pilot of Crew 8

Colonel Edward J. York

Colonel Edward Joseph "Ski" York, born Edward Joseph Cichowski on 16 August 1912, in Batavia, New York, was a man whose life was shaped by his Polish heritage, strong family values, and an unwavering commitment to service. His nickname "Ski" derived from his surname at birth. His parents, Ignatius and Tekla Cichowski, were Polish immigrants who brought with them the rich traditions, language, and cultural values of their homeland. Ignatius, who arrived in the United States in 1904, worked tirelessly to create a stable life for his family, facing the challenges of immigrant life in early twentieth-century America with determination and resilience. Despite the hardships they faced, Ignatius and Tekla instilled in their children the importance of hard work, education, and dedication to their community – values that would form the foundation of Edward's future accomplishments and his distinguished career.

Edward, affectionately known as "Eddy" in his younger years, grew up in a household that blended the old customs of Poland with the opportunities and challenges of American life. The Cichowski family was large, close-knit, and deeply connected to their Polish roots. They honored their traditions, spoke Polish at home, and were active in the local Polish community. Edward grew up with a strong sense of family loyalty and pride, further reinforced by his parents' emphasis on the importance of education and self-discipline.

This upbringing, infused with a mix of Polish cultural heritage and the American ethos of opportunity, later influenced his decision to pursue a military career, where discipline, loyalty, and service were paramount.

The early twentieth century was a period of great change and challenge in the United States, particularly for immigrant families like the Cichowskis. The industrialization of the northeast attracted large numbers of Eastern European immigrants, who settled in towns like Batavia and contributed to the economic and cultural fabric of these communities. However, immigrants often faced prejudice, discrimination, and economic hardship as they tried to build a life in a new and often hostile land. Despite these challenges, the Cichowski family maintained their cultural identity and supported one another in their efforts to succeed in America. They became part of a vibrant Polish-American community that provided a sense of belonging and mutual support, reinforcing the values of hard work, perseverance, and dedication to family.

Edward's early education began at the State Street School in Batavia, New York, later renamed John Kennedy Elementary School. He continued his education at Batavia High School, where he excelled academically and showed an early aptitude for math and mechanics – skills that would later prove invaluable. From a young age, Edward became fascinated by the technological advances, especially in aviation and mechanics, that emerged after the First World War. The rapid development of new technologies and his growing passion for flying fueled his dream of becoming a pilot. Edward spent countless hours reading about aviation and the mechanics involved.

During these formative years, Edward began envisioning a future in the military, possibly in the infantry or the Air Force. The discipline and structured life of a military man appealed to him. After graduating from Batavia High School in 1930, where he was known as an outstanding student with a talent for mathematics, Edward decided to enlist in the U.S. Army. At the time, the United States was still grappling with the effects of the Great Depression, and military service offered young men like Edward a stable career and an opportunity to serve their country. As an enlisted man, he served for three years, gaining valuable experience and adapting to the structured life of a soldier. During this time, Edward was stationed in various locations, including the Chilkoot Barracks in Alaska.

After three years of military service, and aided by paternal support and a recommendation from Senator Hiram Johnson of California, he was admitted to the United States Military Academy at West Point in 1936, where he laid the foundation for a distinguished military career.

Edward Joseph Cichowski later changed his name to Edward J. York after joining the military. This name change was likely due to the challenges faced by people with non-English names at the time, as it was common for individuals to adopt more Americanized names. This decision reflected Edward's desire to fully integrate into American society and perhaps to ease the pronunciation and recognition of his name within the military.

Edward's father, Ignatius, played a crucial role in his son's military ambitions. Ignatius, a man of strong character and a dedication to his family, supported Edward's decision to pursue a military career, recognizing the opportunities it offered for personal growth and service to the country. Ignatius understood the value of hard work and perseverance, having built a life for his family in a new land through sheer determination. He saw in Edward the same qualities that had driven him to succeed, and he encouraged his son to pursue his dreams with the same tenacity.

West Point was one of the most prestigious military institutions in the United States, the pinnacle of military education, and gaining admission was a testament to Edward's academic achievements and his potential as a military leader.

Edward thrived at West Point. The academy's demanding curriculum and strict code of conduct were designed to produce leaders of the highest caliber, and Edward rose to meet that challenge. Initially, he was drawn to the cavalry, a branch of the military with a rich tradition and an appeal to those who admired the romance of mounted service. The image of a cavalry officer, commanding respect and leading men on horseback into battle, was deeply rooted in American military tradition.

However, the practical realities of military life soon became apparent. The cost of cavalry uniforms was prohibitively high at a time when financial considerations were crucial for many cadets, including Edward. Faced with this economic reality, he made a decisive move that would alter the course of his career. He shifted his focus to his true passion: aviation, a field that not only was more affordable in terms of uniform costs but also aligned with his deep-seated interest in flying. This decision marked the beginning of Edward's journey into military aviation.

The transition from cavalry to aviation was more than a practical choice; it reflected Edward's ability to adapt to changing circumstances and seize new opportunities while also fulfilling a lifelong dream. By choosing aviation, Edward entered a field on the cusp of major technological innovation and military strategy, positioning himself to be part of the future of warfare.

Edward undertook flight training in San Antonio, Texas, as part of his preparation to become a pilot in the U.S. Army Air Corps. Specifically, he was sent to Kelly Field, one of the primary pilot training facilities of the time.

On 28 August 1939, Edward married Mary Harper York, a union that would provide him with the emotional and moral support he needed throughout his demanding military career. Mary was a dedicated partner, and together they built a life that balanced the challenges of military service with the joys of family life.

The couple had two children, one daughter and one son, who were a constant source of pride and joy for Edward. Mary's unwavering support was crucial, especially during the most difficult periods of Edward's service. She managed the household with grace and strength, ensuring their children were cared for and that the family remained a stable and loving environment, despite the demands of military life. Mary's resilience and dedication allowed Edward to focus on his duties, knowing that his family was well cared for.

Family life was of the utmost importance to Edward, and despite the demands of his career, he remained involved in the lives of his wife and children. The York family's life was shaped by the unpredictable nature of military service, with frequent moves and long periods of separation. Nevertheless, they maintained a strong family bond, underpinned by mutual respect, love, and a shared sense of duty. Edward's dedication to his family mirrored his dedication to his country, and this balance between personal and professional responsibilities became a defining feature of his character. The York household was one where values such as honor, duty, and service were not just words but guiding principles that shaped every aspect of their lives. Edward's role as a father and husband was just as important to him as his military service, and he took particular pride in the achievements and wellbeing of his family.

After completing his flight training and receiving his commission as an officer, Edward received his first assignment as a pilot of the A-17 and B-18 at March Field, California, from August 1939 to June 1940. This assignment provided him with valuable experience in flying different types of military aircraft, laying the foundation for his future role in more complex missions. He later served at McChord Field, Washington, where he flew B-23 Dragons and B-25 Mitchells until June 1941.

Later, Edward was transferred to Pendleton Field, Oregon, where he continued to serve as a pilot of the B-25 Mitchell in the 95th Bomb

Squadron. In February 1942, while stationed at Pendleton, he volunteered and was selected to participate in the Doolittle Raid. This selection was a testament to Edward's abilities and the trust his superiors placed in him to carry out such a risky operation.

As a captain in the U.S. Army Air Forces, Edward York was chosen as the pilot of the eighth plane to take off during the Doolittle Raid.

Following intensive training at Eglin Field, Florida, the raiders departed from San Francisco aboard the USS *Hornet* on 2 April 1942. After the fleet being spotted by Japanese picket boats, Edward piloted the eighth plane to take off from the *Hornet* at 8:46 am on 18 April 1942, earlier than had been planned, and further away from their target. The B-25 Mitchell bomber he flew bore the USAAF serial number 40-2242 and the NAA factory number 62B-2911. The aircraft had no name.

Despite the challenge posed by the greater distances, Edward York and his crew carried out their mission with determination. Edward quickly realized that his plane was burning more fuel than expected. The carburetors were not properly adjusted, and it became clear that they would not reach their destination in China. The situation was dire, and Edward had to make a crucial decision to ensure the safety of his crew.

Rather than risk crashing into the sea, Edward made the decision to divert to the Soviet Union, hoping to find safe haven there. Although the Soviet Union was technically an ally of the United States, it was not at war with Japan, and the decision to land there was fraught with uncertainty. On their way to the Soviet Union, Edward's crew bombed an alternate target in Japan before making an emergency landing near Vladivostok, Russia, making them the only Doolittle Raiders to land in Soviet territory. The Soviet Union had a non-aggression pact with Japan, so this put the Soviets in a diplomatically delicate position, as openly assisting American airmen could provoke a conflict with Japan, something they wanted to avoid.

Upon arrival, Edward and his crew were taken into custody by Soviet authorities. While they were not mistreated, they were effectively interned for more than a year, as the Soviets adhered strictly to international law regarding the internment of military combatants from a country with which they were not officially at war.

During their internment, Edward and his crew were moved between various locations, including Khabarovsk in the far east of Russia and more remote areas in Central Asia. The living conditions were basic, and the crew had limited freedom, but they were not subjected to harsh treatment. The Soviets ensured that the American airmen received adequate food, shelter, and medical care, though they were cautious about their diplomatic position.

Throughout this period, Edward displayed remarkable leadership and resilience. He kept his crew's morale high despite the uncertainty of their situation. With limited communication with the outside world, the crew had little information about the progress of the war or the likelihood of their release. Yet, Edward remained determined, leading his men and strengthening their camaraderie. His ability to keep his men motivated and focused on the hope of eventual release was a testament to his leadership and deep commitment to his crew.

In 1943, after more than a year in Soviet custody, a secret operation was launched to "allow" Edward and his crew to escape their internment. The operation was discreetly coordinated between the U.S. military and Soviet authorities, with the aim of providing a way for Edward and his men to leave Soviet territory without causing a diplomatic incident. Under the guise of a routine relocation, Edward and his crew were moved to Ashgabat, Turkmenistan, a remote outpost near the Iranian border. From there, they were able to cross into British-controlled Iran, where they finally made contact with American forces and arranged their return to the United States.

The operation required careful planning and was largely kept quiet to avoid diplomatic complications and to maintain the fragile relationship between the Soviet Union and Japan. The crossing into Iran was facilitated by the shifting political dynamics and increasing cooperation between the Allies as the Second World War progressed. This successful maneuver highlighted not only the strong coordination between U.S. and Soviet officials but also the willingness of both parties to collaborate under challenging circumstances.

The plane that Edward and his crew had flown during the Doolittle Raid was retained by the Soviets for research and testing. Over the years, the aircraft was used for various purposes. It was eventually scrapped in 1957 after being used repeatedly for research and routine operations. The successful escape and return of Edward and his crew were celebrated as a diplomatic success, illustrating the complexities of wartime alliances and the subtle maneuvers required to maintain them.

Edward's leadership during this period was crucial. He kept his crew focused and motivated despite the uncertainty surrounding their internment. The experience forged a deep bond among the crew members, characterized by mutual respect and trust, born out of the adversities they had faced together. Their ability to endure their internment and ultimately escape was a testament to their resilience and the effectiveness of Allied cooperation during the war.

Upon their return to the United States, Edward and his crew were hailed as heroes, not only for their role in the Doolittle Raid but also for their resilience and ingenuity during their internment in the Soviet Union. Edward's experience in the Soviet Union was unique among the Doolittle Raiders and added a complex layer to the already extraordinary story of the raid.

After the Doolittle Raid, Edward continued his military career with distinction. He trained on various bombers, including the B-25 Mitchell, B-24 Liberator, and B-17 Flying Fortress, before being assigned to the 483rd Bomb Group in Italy. There, he flew combat missions between March and June 1944, contributing to the Allied war effort in Europe. Edward's experience and expertise made him an invaluable asset during this critical phase of the war, and he played a key role in the strategic bombing campaigns targeting enemy infrastructure and military installations.

From August 1944 to June 1945 he served as an air inspector at Randolph AFB, Texas. His duties included ensuring the readiness and effectiveness of air operations, a role that required meticulous attention to detail. He was then appointed as air attaché in Poland from July 1945 to December 1946, where his fluency in Polish and Russian proved invaluable. His work in Poland, particularly his role in helping to establish a provisional government of national unity, was recognized by the United States, Britain, and the Soviet Union. Edward's ability to navigate the complex political landscape of post-war Poland was a testament to his diplomatic skills and understanding of the region.

After his service in Poland, Edward continued to hold important positions within the U.S. Air Force. From March 1947 to April 1948 he served as commandant of the Air Force Officer Training School at the San Antonio Aviation Cadet Center, later renamed Lackland AFB, Texas. In this role, he was responsible for training the next generation of Air Force officers, imparting values of leadership, discipline, and service. He then served as air attaché in Denmark from August 1948 to February 1950, before becoming chief of the Air Force section for the Military Assistance Advisory Group in Copenhagen, Denmark, from February 1950 to June 1951.

Edward's career continued with his attendance at the Air War College at Maxwell AFB, Alabama, from which he graduated in June 1952. The Air War College was the premier educational institution for the U.S. Air Force, and his participation there marked him as one of the top officers in the Air Force. He then became chief of the air attaché branch at the headquarters of the U.S. Air Force in the Pentagon, serving until June 1955. In this role, he oversaw the activities of air attachés stationed around the world, ensuring they effectively represented U.S. interests and gathered valuable intelligence.

From June 1955 to August 1958, Edward served as deputy chief of staff for planning at the headquarters of the Military Air Transport Service at Andrews AFB, Maryland. His next assignment was as chief of staff for the headquarters of the Western Transport Air Force at Travis AFB, California, until August 1960. These positions placed Edward at the heart of strategic planning and logistics operations for the Air Force, where he played a crucial role in ensuring that the U.S. military could respond quickly and effectively to global challenges.

Edward's final military assignments included commanding an ICBM Site Activation Task Force at Larson AFB, Washington, from August 1960 to November 1962, and serving as chief of staff at the headquarters of the U.S. Air Force Security Service at Kelly AFB, Texas, from November 1962 to June 1966. The ICBM Site Activation Task Force was responsible for overseeing the deployment of intercontinental ballistic missiles for the U.S. Air Force, a critical component of the country's nuclear deterrent during the Cold War. His leadership in this role was essential to the successful deployment of these strategic weapons. He then served as deputy commander at the headquarters of the U.S. Air Force Security Service until his retirement on 2 September 1966.

Edward Joseph York passed away on 31 August 1984 in San Antonio, Texas. He was buried with full military honors at Fort Sam Houston National Cemetery. His life story, from his beginnings as the son of Polish immigrants to his role in one of the Second World War's most daring missions, remains a powerful example of what it means to serve with honor and dedication. His legacy is a lasting tribute to the courage and sacrifice of those who fought to protect the freedoms we enjoy today, and his memory continues to inspire new generations of servicemen and women.

Edward York's life is not only a story of individual achievement but also a reflection of broader historical forces that shaped the twentieth century. His story is intertwined with the immigrant experience in America, the rise of military aviation, and the global conflicts that defined his time. In honoring him, we recognize not only his individual achievements but also the collective efforts of all those who served during the Second World War. His story is a part of the larger narrative of the Greatest Generation, a generation that faced unprecedented challenges with courage and determination. The lessons learned from his life and career are as relevant today as they were during his time, reminding us of the importance of service, sacrifice, and the enduring values that define our nation.

Pilot of Crew 9

Lieutenant Colonel Harold F. Watson

Lieutenant Colonel Harold Francis "Doc" Watson was born on 3 April 1916 in Buffalo, New York, to Harold David Watson and Frances Josephine Urban. The Watson family was a typical early twentieth-century American family, with values of hard work, education, and personal responsibility. Harold's father, Harold David Watson, was a dedicated and hardworking man who instilled in his son the importance of integrity and perseverance. His mother, Frances Josephine Urban, was a caring and supportive figure, ensuring that her children were raised with strong moral and ethical values.

During Harold's early years, the Watson family moved to West Hartford, Connecticut, a move that would have a significant impact on his upbringing. West Hartford, a suburban community known for its excellent schools and strong sense of community, provided a supportive environment for Harold's development. Here, Harold attended elementary school and spent his formative years growing up in a household that emphasized education, personal responsibility, and the development of leadership qualities. These early influences would shape his future career and the way he approached life's challenges.

Harold Watson attended William H. Hall High School in West Hartford, where he quickly distinguished himself both academically and athletically. He was known for his sharp intellect and strong work ethic, consistently achieving high grades in his classes. His academic success was matched by his athletic achievements, where he not only displayed physical prowess but also demonstrated strategic thinking and leadership skills. Harold actively participated in various school sports teams, excelling through his combination of natural athletic ability and an understanding of teamwork and strategy. His peers and teachers recognized him as a natural leader, someone who could inspire others and bring out the best in his teammates.

During his time at William H. Hall High School, Harold developed a reputation as reliable, disciplined, and committed to his goals. These traits were encouraged by the environment in which he grew up: a community that valued education, hard work, and moral integrity. Harold's ability to balance academic with extracurricular activities showcased his time-management skills and his capacity to handle multiple responsibilities, qualities that would serve him well in his future military career.

After living in West Hartford for about ten years, Harold later moved to Arlington, Virginia. His time in West Hartford had been crucial in shaping his character, and he had become an integral part of the local community, known for his involvement in school and extracurricular activities. The move to Arlington marked a new chapter in Harold's life, characterized by both personal and professional growth. Arlington, with its proximity to the nation's capital, offered new opportunities and challenges that allowed Harold to further develop his leadership skills and continue his commitment to public service.

Harold Watson's academic journey continued at Norwich University in Northfield, Vermont. This university, founded in 1819 by Captain Alden Partridge, is known as the birthplace of the Reserve Officers Training Corps (ROTC) program. Partridge's vision of the "American system of education" integrated traditional liberal arts with civil engineering and military science, with the goal of producing well-rounded leaders equipped for both military and civilian roles.

At Norwich, Harold graduated in Science and Literature, fields that reflected his broad intellectual interests. He was not only a diligent student but also an active member of the university community. His involvement in a wide range of extracurricular activities helped him develop skills that would prove invaluable throughout his military career. Notably, his membership in the university's polo team showcased his precision and coordination in a demanding and competitive sport. The team was known for its strong performances, and Harold's contributions were essential to their success.

In addition to his athletic achievements, Harold was a member of the Theta Chi fraternity. His involvement in the fraternity highlighted his sociable nature and his dedication to building strong, lasting relationships with his peers. His leadership qualities were further recognized by his election as class president and his role as president of the Maroon Key, an honor society for student leaders and high achievers. These positions allowed Harold to refine his leadership skills and work closely with others to achieve common goals.

After completing his studies at Norwich University, Harold Watson sought to further his education at the prestigious Virginia Military Institute (VMI) in Lexington, Virginia, an institution renowned for its rigorous military training and academic discipline. For Harold, VMI represented an ideal environment to sharpen his leadership abilities, refine his intellectual pursuits, and fortify his commitment to a career in military service. The strict, disciplined culture of VMI not only aligned with his personal ambitions but also provided him with the structured foundation necessary for a successful future in the U.S. military.

At VMI, Harold thrived academically, consistently demonstrating a passion for learning and an aptitude for excelling in both military sciences and liberal arts. VMI's unique approach to education, which seamlessly combined academic rigor with military discipline, suited Harold's ambition to become a well-rounded leader. The demanding curriculum sharpened his analytical thinking and problem-solving abilities, both of which would prove invaluable during his military career. The intense focus on personal responsibility, time management, and teamwork further developed the leadership skills he had begun to cultivate during his time at Norwich.

While his academic success at VMI was noteworthy, Harold's dedication to physical fitness and competitive spirit stood out just as prominently. He took full advantage of the school's athletic opportunities, participating in various sports that tested his endurance, resilience, and discipline. A member of the boxing team, Harold displayed not only physical strength but also mental toughness, skills that are critical both in the boxing ring and in the theater of war. His involvement in the rifle team demonstrated his precision, focus, and composure – traits that would later be essential in high-stakes military situations.

Harold's participation in track and field further highlighted his dedication to physical fitness and perseverance. Track and field required Harold to push his physical limits and endure intense training, much like what would be required of him in his future military career. Additionally, Harold's experience on the football team, a sport that emphasizes teamwork, communication, and strategic thinking, provided him with valuable lessons in camaraderie and leadership under pressure. These qualities, developed on the football field, would later prove indispensable in his capacity as a military officer.

Throughout his time at VMI, Harold displayed an unwavering commitment to both his academic and athletic endeavors, and this dedication did not go unnoticed. His professors, coaches, and peers alike recognized Harold's leadership potential and respected his disciplined approach to both intellectual and physical challenges. His ability to balance academics and athletics mirrored the balance required in military life, where officers are expected to manage a range of responsibilities with precision and discipline.

VMI's military training further enhanced Harold's leadership skills, reinforcing the values of duty, honor, and service. His experience with military drills, tactical training, and the school's emphasis on military tradition and strict discipline prepared him to lead others in the complex and high-stress situations he would encounter in the years to come. The sense of brotherhood and mutual respect cultivated among the cadets at VMI also played a significant role in shaping Harold's leadership style. He learned the importance of loyalty, trust, and unity – qualities that would serve him well when leading troops in combat.

Norwich had instilled in Harold a strong intellectual foundation, while VMI honed his tactical expertise and leadership abilities. The combination of these two educational experiences ensured that Harold entered his military career as a well-rounded, disciplined, and capable leader. By the time Harold graduated from VMI, he had developed a sense of duty and a clear vision for his future in the military. His education and experiences at VMI had prepared him not only for the challenges of military service but also for the leadership roles he would soon assume. Equipped with the training necessary to succeed, Harold was ready to embark on a distinguished career in the U.S. Army Air Corps.

Harold Watson's military career began on 6 November 1939, when he enrolled in the Aviation Cadet Program of the U.S. Army Air Corps. This decision marked the start of a long and distinguished career in military aviation. Harold excelled throughout the intense and demanding training program, demonstrating the discipline, determination, and technical skills required to succeed in this challenging environment.

On 9 July 1940, he officially entered the U.S. Army, signifying his entry into the U.S. Army Air Corps, which would later become part of the U.S. Army Air Forces during the Second World War. On 12 April 1941, Harold was commissioned as a lieutenant after earning his pilot wings at Kelly Field in San Antonio, Texas. This milestone, achieved on 31 August 1940, marked the official beginning of his career as a military pilot.

On 2 April 1941, shortly before officially beginning his military career, Harold Watson married Geneva Marie Gitchell in Tacoma, Washington. This union marked the beginning of a lifelong partnership that endured through the many challenges of the Second World War and beyond. Their marriage was based on mutual respect, love, and a shared commitment to their country. Geneva's strength and resilience would be a source of comfort and stability for Harold throughout his career, especially in the most challenging moments of the war. Geneva Marie Gitchell worked as a teacher. As the wife of Lieutenant Harold F. Watson, she managed to balance her professional career in education with the challenges of life as a military spouse during the Second World War, supporting her husband and contributing to her community through her role in education. The couple had two daughters.

The Watsons eventually settled in Arlington, Virginia, where they would raise their family. Although much of Harold's life was consumed by his military duties, he always made time for his family, ensuring that they had a close and supportive bond. His experiences in the military, especially during the war, reinforced his appreciation for the importance of family, and he strove to instill the same values of integrity, hard work, and service to others in his children.

Harold Watson's early assignments in the U.S. Army Air Corps included flying B-18 Bolo and B-23 Dragon aircraft. The B-18 Bolo and B-23 Dragon were both early American bombers, and by flying them, Harold gained valuable experience that he would need for the transition to more complex and demanding aircraft.

Harold later transitioned to flying the B-25 Mitchell and he was assigned to the 34th Bomb Squadron of the 17th Bomb Group, initially stationed at McChord Field in Washington and later at Pendleton Army Airfield in Oregon. These assignments allowed

Harold to further hone his piloting skills and prepare for the critical missions that lay ahead.

In February 1942, Harold volunteered for the Doolittle Raid, and he soon found himself in Florida, training for this secret operation. The Doolittle Raiders trained intensively at Eglin Field, but as mentioned before, the men only discovered the true nature of the mission when on the deck of the USS *Hornet* after the task force departed from San Francisco on 2 April 1942.

After being spotted by a Japanese picket boat, the sixteen B-25s on the deck of the *Hornet* were left with little choice but to set off on their mission earlier than planned. On 18 April 1942, Harold Watson took off at 8:50 am as the pilot of the ninth aircraft from the *Hornet*. His B-25 Mitchell bomber, named "Whirling Dervish", carried USAAF serial number 40-2303 and NAA manufacturer serial number 62B-2972.

During the flight to Tokyo, Crew 9 encountered a fuel leak where the lower gun turret had been replaced by a fuel bag. Despite this problem, they made contingency plans in case they ran out of fuel over the sea. They agreed that if they ran out of fuel, they would attempt to ditch near a small boat, take control of the boat, and sail to the Chinese coast. Fortunately, this action was not necessary.

Crew 9's mission was to target the Mitsubishi Aircraft Works, a key factory for the production of military aircraft, as well as other industrial areas and warehouses that were essential to Japan's war effort. The primary goal was to damage these strategic locations, send a psychological message to Japan, and boost American morale. Despite the risks, the mission succeeded in demonstrating Japan's vulnerability to American air strikes.

After their bombing, Harold and his crew found themselves in a dangerous situation due to low fuel levels. They were forced to bail out over China. They landed in the mountains among the Chinese mountain dwellers. During the parachute jump, Harold fractured his arm and shoulder because his parachute harness was too small, causing his injury when the parachute opened. Despite his injury, Harold managed to evade capture with the help of Chinese villagers and resistance fighters. He and his crew members ended up in the mountains and were transported via Hengyang to Chongqing with the help of the local Chinese population.

Harold was brought to Chongqing, the wartime capital of Free China, by litter and airplane, as his injury prevented him from walking. The crew's journey through enemy-occupied territory and rough terrain was harrowing, but by early May 1942, they safely reached Chongqing. There, they reunited with other members of the Doolittle Raid and were eventually evacuated to the United States.

Harold, one of the most seriously injured survivors of the raid, became a patient at Walter Reed Hospital. He remained there until July 1943, after which he resumed his service in various posts across the United States. His injury, a severe and complicated arm fracture, required advanced medical care, but Harold's determination and resilience helped him recover.

Following his recovery, Harold was assigned to give lectures about his experiences in the Doolittle Raid across the United States until October 1943. These lectures were an important part of his recovery period, as they allowed him to share the lessons he had learned from the mission and inspire others.

After this lecture tour, Harold served as base operations officer at Gowen Field, Idaho, from November 1943 to April 1944. This role marked his return to active duty and allowed him to apply his extensive experience and knowledge to managing base operations. His next assignment was as retention officer in Atlantic City, New Jersey, from April 1944 to October 1945. In this role, Harold was responsible for managing and improving retention efforts, ensuring that the military maintained a strong and capable force during a crucial period in the war.

Harold continued his military career, serving in various roles across the United States. From October 1945 to June 1947, he served as administrative officer, assistant base adjutant, and base adjutant with the 268th, 201st, and 200th Army Air Force Base Units at Peterson Field, Colorado. These roles involved significant administrative responsibilities, requiring Harold to oversee the efficient operation of the base and support the personnel under his command.

In June 1947, Harold was appointed base adjutant with the 203rd Base Unit at Spokane Field, Washington, where he served until September 1947, after which he joined the staff of the 92nd Bomb Group at Spokane, serving from September to October 1947.

His next position was as a B-29 Superfortress pilot and deputy commander of the 325th Bomb Squadron of the 92nd Bomb Group at Spokane AFB, from October 1947 to April 1948. He then served as chief of the collection division, chief of the operations division, chief of the operations center, and assistant chief of the special projects division at the 1009th Special Weapons Squadron at Bolling AFB, Washington, D.C., from April 1948 to July 1952. This unit was responsible for worldwide detection of nuclear detonations, a task of great strategic importance during the early years of the Cold War. Harold's role in this unit emphasized his expertise in operations and his ability to manage complex and sensitive missions.

In July 1952, Harold attended the Air Command and Staff College at Maxwell AFB, Alabama. This prestigious institution provided advanced training to military officers to prepare them for higher command and leadership roles. Harold completed the course in December 1952, further enhancing his qualifications and readiness for future assignments.

After completing his studies at the Air Command and Staff College, Harold was admitted to the hospital at Maxwell AFB from January to March 1953 to receive treatment for complications relating to injury sustained when parachuting from his aircraft during the Doolittle

Raid. His time in the hospital was a period of recovery and reflection, during which he prepared to return to active duty. After his recovery, Harold served as a B-47 Stratojet pilot and staff officer for operations with the 308th Bomb Wing at Hunter AFB, Georgia, from March to April 1953. He then served as director of personnel with the 804th Air Base Group at Hunter AFB from April 1953 to April 1954.

Harold's career continued to progress with his appointment as division chief with the director of targets at the headquarters of the Far East Air Forces in Tokyo, Japan, from April 1954 to October 1955. In this role, Harold was responsible for overseeing the planning and execution of target operations, a crucial aspect of military strategy in the Far East during the Cold War.

After his service in Japan, Harold returned to the United States, where he served as a staff officer for operations with the 805th Air Base Group at Barksdale AFB, Louisiana, from October 1955 to June 1956. His next assignment was as a division chief in the inspection division of the office of the inspector general at the headquarters of the 2nd Air Force at Barksdale AFB, from June 1956 to February 1957.

In March 1957, Harold was appointed as base personnel officer and later as director of military personnel with the 811th and 31st Air Base Groups at Turner AFB, Georgia. He served in these roles until June 1958, after which he was appointed director of personnel with the 506th Tactical Fighter Wing at Tinker AFB, Oklahoma. Harold served in this capacity from June 1958 to April 1959, overseeing personnel management and ensuring the effective operation of the wing.

In April 1959, Harold was transferred to George AFB, California, where he served in various roles, including director of material, base inspector general, director of personnel, and executive officer with the 831st Air Base Group. He served in these capacities until his retirement from the Air Force on 1 November 1961. In his later years,

Harold lived in California, where he remained involved in veterans' activities and shared his experiences with younger generations.

Lieutenant Colonel Harold F. Watson passed away on 14 September 1991 in Inglewood, California. After his death, he was cremated, and the exact location of his ashes is unknown. His legacy as a decorated military officer, particularly for his role in the Doolittle Raid, continues to be honored and remembered. His death marked the end of a distinguished life filled with significant military service and dedication. Harold's contributions during the Second World War, especially as a member of the Doolittle Raid, are remembered and his courage, leadership, and dedication to his country left a lasting impression on those who served with him and on the history of the U.S. military.

Pilot of Crew 10

Lieutenant Colonel Richard O. Joyce

Lieutenant Colonel Richard Outcalt "Dick" Joyce was born on 28 September 1919 in Lincoln, Nebraska, USA. His childhood unfolded during a time of significant global and domestic challenges, from the aftermath of the First World War to the deep Depression of the 1930s. These events shaped the environment in which Richard grew up, and the values instilled in him.

Richard's father, Robert M. Joyce, was a bank manager, a position that brought both stability and considerable responsibility during the economic turmoil of the 1930s. The financial turbulence of that time undoubtedly influenced Robert's career and, by extension, the life of his family. In an era when many faced economic hardships, the Joyce family maintained a certain level of stability, though this came with the pressures and uncertainties inherent to the banking sector. These experiences likely taught young Richard the importance of resilience, financial prudence, and hard work, lessons that would serve him well throughout his life.

Richard's mother, Jessie W. Outcalt, was a homemaker and played a central role in the Joyce family. Her responsibilities went beyond the usual household tasks; she was the emotional anchor of the family, ensuring that her children grew up in a nurturing and supportive environment. Jessie's dedication to her family and her husband's career during these difficult times was likely a source of strength for

Richard, helping him develop his character and instilling in him a strong sense of duty and responsibility. The Joyce family was close-knit, a unity reinforced by shared experiences and the strong moral and ethical values that Robert and Jessie instilled in their children. Despite the challenges of the Great Depression, the resilience and unity of the family provided Richard with a solid foundation during his formative years.

Richard's education began at Prescott Elementary School in Lincoln, where he received a basic education that laid the groundwork for his later academic and professional achievements. The curriculum at Prescott Elementary likely included the core subjects of reading, writing, arithmetic, and social studies, areas that not only encouraged academic growth but also helped Richard develop a broader understanding of the world around him. It was probably during these early years that Richard began developing the interests and curiosity that would shape his future.

When Richard moved on to Lincoln High School, where he graduated in 1937, his academic journey continued to blossom. High school provided a broad education, including subjects like English, mathematics, science, history, and physical education. In addition to core subjects, Lincoln High offered various extracurricular activities, giving Richard the opportunity to explore different interests. Although there is little documentation of his participation in extracurricular activities, it is likely that Richard was involved in programs that helped him develop his leadership skills and broaden his horizons. He earned a diploma in business administration. The high school period was a time of significant personal growth and development for Richard, marked by academic success and a growing awareness of the broader world, a world that was rapidly changing with the approach of the Second World War.

In 1937, Richard enrolled at the University of Nebraska, Lincoln, marking a new chapter in his academic and personal life. His time at the university was characterized by a dedication to academic pursuits and active participation in campus life. This period of study gave Richard a greater understanding of various subjects and exposed him to new ideas and perspectives. The late 1930s were a time of considerable global tensions, with technological advancements and aviation drawing worldwide attention. These developments likely influenced Richard's growing interest in flying, an interest that would soon become a central part of his life.

While studying at the University of Nebraska, Richard joined the Nebraska National Guard, where he served from 13 July 1937 to 13 June 1938. Later, on 27 July 1940, he joined the Aviation Cadet Program of the U.S. Army Air Corps. This decision marked the beginning of his military career and a new chapter in his life. When he enlisted during a time of global uncertainty, Richard knew he was joining a force that could potentially become involved in a significant conflict. The rigorous training that followed tested his physical and mental endurance, preparing him for the challenges ahead.

On 15 March 1941, Richard was commissioned as a lieutenant and received his pilot's wings at Kelly Field, Texas. His dedication was evident when he was promoted to lieutenant. This promotion came just months before the U.S. entered the Second World War, following the attack on Pearl Harbor on 7 December 1941.

As a newly commissioned officer, Richard was thrust into a world of unprecedented challenges and opportunities. His education and the values instilled in him during his upbringing would prove invaluable as he navigated the complexities of military service during one of the most tumultuous periods in history. His early service saw him stationed at McChord Field, Washington, and Pendleton Field, Oregon, where he served as a B-25 Mitchell pilot with the 89th Reconnaissance Squadron of the 17th Bomb Group.

In February 1942, Richard volunteered for the Doolittle Raid – despite not knowing what the mission would entail. This would only become apparent once he had completed training at Eglin Field, Florida, and was already aboard the USS *Hornet*.

The task force responsible for bringing the B-25s to a launch point approximately 400 miles from Japan consisted of two aircraft carriers, fourteen support ships, and two submarines.

Having departed from San Francisco on 2 April 1942, the decision to start the mission early was forced on them after the American task force was spotted by a Japanese picket boat. On 18 April, Lieutenant Richard O. Joyce piloted the tenth aircraft to take off from the *Hornet* at 8:53 am. His B-25 Mitchell bomber, unnamed and identified by USAAF serial number 40-2250 and NAA manufacturer number 62B-2919, took him and his crew on a dangerous mission to bomb Japan.

Richard's aircraft targeted key military and industrial facilities in Tokyo and surrounding areas, including docks, factories, and other critical infrastructure. Although the raid was primarily symbolic in its immediate effect, it had a profound psychological impact.

As Richard's aircraft approached the target area, it encountered anti-aircraft fire over Tokyo Bay, a significant challenge given the already dangerous nature of the mission. The fire intensified as they neared their targets in Tokyo, with shells exploding around the bomber in a concentrated effort to bring the plane down. Richard, showing exceptional skill and calm under pressure, managed to evade the heavy fire by increasing the plane's speed and executing a series of sharp evasive maneuvers. His actions not only protected his crew but also ensured that the bombs were dropped on their intended targets, contributing to the overall success of the raid.

Despite the successful bombings, the dangers were far from over. The crew had to steer their aircraft out of the defended area, knowing that their fuel was nearly depleted and there were limited options for safe landing sites. Their original plan to land in friendly Chinese territory had been jeopardized by the unexpected need to launch earlier than planned. This meant that the crew had to stretch their resources to the limit, flying under uncertain conditions in the hope of reaching safety.

As they neared the Chinese coast, the fuel situation became critical. With no other option, the crew prepared to bail out. Richard led the crew in bailing out over Chinese territory. They parachuted into the unknown and landed in difficult, remote terrain. Richard himself landed on a steep mountainside, alone and surrounded by mist and rain. Despite the isolation and challenging conditions, Richard's training and determination helped him survive the night.

> I landed rather abruptly because I couldn't gauge when I was going to land. I wasn't far from the plane, but I realized I was on a rather steep slope and I could hardly see anything due to the mist and rain. I was unharmed. I unbuckled myself from the harness, grabbed my musette bag, and wrapped myself in my parachute in an attempt to sleep and stay warm and dry. The next morning, it was still misty, and once it cleared enough to see something, I began walking toward the wreckage of the plane. I had to climb over the mountain I had landed on.

After a difficult trek, Richard reached the wreckage of his plane, near what is now the Xin'anjiang Reservoir, where he met friendly Chinese villagers who had come to the crash site. Although the plane was completely lost, Richard was relieved to be alive and to have fulfilled his part in the daring mission, which would later be hailed as a turning point in the war.

> I had landed on a high mountain with a steep slope full of rocks and cliffs. I realized I was very lucky not to be seriously injured. The plane was only about a mile and a half away, but it took me four hours to get there. When

> I reached the crash site, which was also very high in the mountains, I found several Chinese people searching through the wreckage. I called out to them and made it clear that I was an American. They were friendly to me. The plane had smashed into the mountainside and was scattered and burned over a wide area. I couldn't salvage anything from the wreckage. It was a total destruction.

Richard's journey through China from 19 April to 4 May 1942 was a story of resilience and survival. On 19 April, he began an escape on foot with a Chinese farmer, avoiding Japanese forces. The rugged terrain and the risk of discovery made the journey grueling. After a day of walking, they encountered Chinese soldiers who initially detained them to verify Richard's identity. Once confirmed, the soldiers helped Richard travel to Tunxi, where difficult landscapes and poor roads added further challenges.

In Tunxi, Richard and his companion switched to the train, a relatively safer and faster means of transportation. The train took them through hilly areas to Tangxi and then to Jinhua and Quzhou, where they constantly faced the threat of Japanese patrols. Quzhou offered a brief respite to plan the next phase of their escape. On 27 April 1942, Richard, accompanied by locals, took the train to Ningbo, evading the dangers of war-damaged infrastructure and enemy patrols.

From Ningbo, Richard traveled by bus to Hengyang, a three-day journey through areas heavily controlled by Japanese forces. The constant looming danger required continuous vigilance. Upon arrival in Hengyang on 2 May, Richard found an opportunity to arrange a flight to Chongqing, the wartime capital of Free China. Despite the risks of flying through Japanese-patrolled airspace, he arrived in Chongqing on 4 May.

Chongqing marked the end of Richard's perilous journey. It served as a refuge for the Doolittle Raid survivors, allowing them to regroup and plan their return to the United States. Richard's escape through enemy territory was made possible by his determination and the bravery of local Chinese civilians and soldiers who risked their lives to assist him.

The Doolittle Raid had demonstrated that the United States was capable of striking back, even in the darkest hours of the war. For Richard, the raid was a defining moment in his life, a moment that would forever link his name to an act of extraordinary bravery and strategic significance. His family, aware of the immense risks he had taken, was undoubtedly proud of his accomplishments.

After the raid, Richard returned to the China-Burma-India theater, where he was assigned to the 22nd Bomb Squadron. As a major, he carried out numerous combat missions, demonstrating skill and bravery under enemy fire. The 22nd Bomb Squadron played a crucial role within the U.S. Army Air Forces and was often called upon to carry out challenging and dangerous missions in various theaters of war. Richard's role as a B-25 pilot involved flying over enemy territory, dropping bombs on strategic targets, and providing support to ground troops, all while navigating enemy airspace and constantly facing the threat of enemy fire.

In addition to his combat duties, Richard also served as a ferry pilot, a role in which he transported aircraft from one location to another, often over long distances and under challenging conditions. As a ferry pilot at the headquarters of the 10th Air Force, Richard was responsible for delivering B-25s and other aircraft where they were most needed, contributing to the operational readiness of the Air Force.

After completing his assignments abroad, Richard returned to the United States in December 1942. His extensive experience in combat and ferry missions made him well-suited for leadership roles within the U.S. Army Air Forces. In January 1943, Richard was appointed assistant officer at the headquarters of III Bomber Command at MacDill Field, Florida. The role involved operational planning, including coordinating and executing bombing missions. At MacDill Field, Richard played a key role in overseeing the preparation and execution of operational strategies, ensuring that bombers were ready for their missions.

In July 1944, Richard transitioned to a new role as director of training at the 357th Army Air Force Base Unit at Kellogg Field, Michigan. Training was a crucial component of the U.S. Army Air Forces' strategy, as the rapid expansion of the Air Force required a steady stream of well-trained pilots and crews. Richard's role as director of training involved overseeing the instruction and preparation of these new Air Force personnel, ensuring that they possessed the skills and knowledge necessary for battle.

From September 1944 to May 1945, Richard continued his leadership in training as director of training at the 381st Army Air Force Base Unit in Marianna, Florida. In this position, he was responsible for a major training facility, ensuring the development and implementation of training programs to prepare Air Force personnel for the challenges of war. His efforts in Marianna contributed to the readiness and effectiveness of the U.S. Army Air Forces during the final phase of the Second World War.

In May 1945, after the war in Europe, Richard was transferred to Moody Field, Georgia, where he served as director of training and operations at the 140th Army Air Force Base Unit. In this role, Richard continued his work in training and took on additional responsibilities related to the overall operational readiness of the unit. His leadership ensured that both the training programs and operational capabilities of the unit remained at the highest level as the war neared its end. Richard's service at Moody Field lasted until November 1945, when he went on leave as the war officially ended.

Richard married his first wife, Eloise Jean DeLacy, in 1946, after the war. Later in life, he married Drusilla Dunhaver Baker in 1964. He had five children with Eloise and two stepchildren with Drusilla.

Following the end of the Second World War, Richard transitioned from active duty to civilian life. On 10 March 1946, he officially left active duty, marking the end of his direct involvement with the U.S. Army Air Forces. However, his dedication to his country did not end with his active service. Richard remained active in the Air Force Reserve and continued to contribute to the nation's defense. He stayed in the reserve until 13 May 1955, when he received an honorable discharge, formally ending his military career.

After his retirement from the Air Force Reserve, Richard returned to civilian life. Although he no longer wore a uniform, the values of service, discipline, and dedication that had guided him throughout his military career continued to influence his life. He worked for Wholesale Hardware Company, a hardware store in Lincoln, Nebraska, founded in 1900 by his father. The store became a well-known establishment in the community, supplying hardware and related goods to customers for many years.

Richard also had a connection with the Lincoln airport in Nebraska, where he became the airport manager after the Second World War. His role in civil aviation after his military service continued to reflect his commitment to aviation. As airport manager, Richard applied the leadership and organizational skills he had honed during his military career and contributed to the growth and development of the airport.

Like many veterans of the Doolittle Raid, Richard likely participated in veteran reunions, community events, and activities related to commemorating the raid and honoring the sacrifices of those involved. The Doolittle Raiders were honored and celebrated for their bravery and contributions during the war, and Richard was part of that legacy.

Richard O. Joyce passed away on 13 February 1983 and was buried at Wyuka Cemetery in Lincoln, Nebraska. His name is remembered on the Wall of Honor at the Steven F. Udvar-Hazy Center of the National Air and Space Museum in Chantilly, Virginia, near Washington D.C.

His name is listed on the seventh panel, recognizing individuals who made significant contributions to aviation and space, whether through military service, as aviation pioneers, or in other capacities.

The story of Lieutenant Colonel Richard Joyce is one of dedication, leadership, and unwavering commitment to duty. His service as a B-25 pilot, ferry pilot, and leader in training new Air Force personnel played a vital role in the success of the U.S. Army Air Forces during the Second World War. As we remember Lieutenant Colonel Joyce, we honor the sacrifices and contributions of all who served during the Second World War. His life and career serve as a reminder of the importance of duty, the value of leadership, and the impact that one person can have on the course of history. The legacy of Lieutenant Colonel Joyce lives on in the generations of Air Force personnel he helped train and in the lasting freedom he helped secure.

Richard Joyce and fellow raider Donald E. Fitzmaurice (Crew 7), were inducted posthumously into the Nebraska Aviation Hall of Fame in 1997.

Pilot of Crew 11

Colonel Charles Ross Greening

"I've always wanted to fly airplanes. I saw my first one when I was four. I grabbed my tricycle and gave chase, not realizing the futility of catching that fascinating machine."

Colonel Charles Ross Greening was born on 12 November 1914 in Carroll, Iowa, United States. He was the son of Charles William Greening, born on 26 July 1882 in Grand Meadow, Mower, Minnesota, and Olive Jewell Ross, born on 27 February 1888 in Earl Park, Benton, Indiana. His parents were married on 22 November 1911. Colonel Greening spent his early years in Montana, a region known for its vast plains and rugged landscapes, which undoubtedly shaped his early experiences and character.

Montana in the early twentieth century was a land of opportunities and challenges, where a pioneering spirit and self-reliance were essential. The Greening family, like many others, sought to build a life in this frontier state. Ross's father, Charles, was a man of diverse interests and occupations. He was not only a bank employee but also a state senator and cattle rancher, managing banks in various small towns across Montana, including Miles City, Roundup, Hardin, and Melstone. These roles reflected Montana's multifaceted economy at the time, a mix of agriculture, livestock farming, and emerging financial services.

Growing up in such an environment, young Ross was instilled with the values of hard work, perseverance, and a deep connection to the land. His father's involvement in politics and banking gave Ross a broader perspective on the challenges and opportunities facing rural America at the time, particularly as the Great Depression began to take hold. The economic hardships that plagued the nation in the 1920s and 1930s had a profound impact on the Greening family, as it did on many others in the region. The collapse of rural banks due to the Depression forced the family to relocate to Tacoma, Washington, in 1925.

This move marked a significant transition in Ross's life. Tacoma, with its bustling port and growing industries, was a stark contrast to the vast rural expanses of Montana. The urban environment offered new opportunities and experiences, but it also meant that Ross had to adapt to a different lifestyle. Despite these changes, Ross's early exposure to aviation in Montana would have a decisive influence on his life. In June 1921, when he was just 6 years old, his parents took him to an airshow at a field near their home in Miles City. It was there that Ross, along with his older sister Shirley, took his first flight. This experience sparked a lifelong passion for aviation that would ultimately define his career.

Ross's fascination with flying was further fueled by attending a parachute jump by Charles A. Lindbergh a few years later. Lindbergh, who would later become famous for his solo transatlantic flight, was a symbol of the daring and adventurous spirit of early aviation. For Ross, these early encounters with aviation were more than just exciting experiences; they were the seeds of a dream that would eventually lead him to the skies as a military pilot.

After moving to Tacoma, Ross continued his education and attended Lincoln High School. Tacoma, located on the shores of Puget Sound, was a city with a rich industrial heritage, including shipbuilding and railroads, which contributed to its growth in the early twentieth century. The city also had a burgeoning aviation community, with the nearby McChord Field, now McChord Air Force Base, developing into a major military airbase in the years leading up to the Second World War.

At Lincoln High School in Tacoma, Ross was an active and athletic student. He participated in various sports, including American football and track and field, where he particularly excelled in javelin throwing. These activities not only kept him physically fit but also taught him the importance of discipline, teamwork, and perseverance.

Ross's academic interests were broad, and he demonstrated a particular aptitude for the arts. This was somewhat unusual for someone with such a strong inclination toward sports and aviation, but it highlighted his diverse talents and interests. He would later combine his artistic skills with his military career in ways that were both innovative and inspiring.

After graduating from high school, Ross enrolled at Washington State College (now Washington State University) in Pullman, Washington. The college, situated in the rolling hills of the Palouse region, was known for its strong programs in agriculture, engineering, and military science. Here, Ross pursued a bachelor's degree in fine arts with minors in physical education and military science. This combination of studies reflected his varied interests and his desire to develop both his creative and physical abilities.

During his time as a student in Washington, Ross Greening was so eager to attend a major airshow that he decided to hitchhike to get there.

In the 1930s, airshows were major events showcasing the latest developments in aviation. For an aspiring pilot like Ross, missing one was simply not an option. Unable to afford transportation to the airshow, Ross chose to hitchhike to ensure he wouldn't miss the event. This adventurous decision demonstrated his dedication to aviation and his determination to do whatever it took to experience it firsthand.

In the summers of 1933 and 1934, during his first and second years at university, he embarked on a journey that would significantly broaden his horizons. He traveled aboard the SS *President Cleveland*, a cruise ship that visited several cities in the Far East, including Yokohama, Kobe, Shanghai, Hong Kong, and Manila. This experience exposed him to various cultures and the growing geopolitical tensions in the region, particularly as Japan's imperial ambitions began to unfold.

Ross's trips to the Far East were not just youthful adventures; they gave him an early glimpse into the global dynamics that would later shape his military career. The increasing influence of Japan in Asia, coupled with rising tensions in Europe, were early signs of the global conflict that would erupt a few years later.

After graduating from Washington State College in 1936 with a bachelor's degree in fine arts, Ross took a significant step toward realizing his dream of becoming a pilot. On 23 June 1936, he enrolled in the U.S. Army Air Corps' Aviation Cadet Program, the precursor to the U.S. Air Force. This program was designed to train young men to become pilots and officers in the rapidly growing air arm of the U.S. Army.

The U.S. Army Air Corps was undergoing significant changes during this period. The introduction of faster, more powerful aircraft and the growing recognition of the strategic importance of airpower drove the expansion and modernization of the Air Corps. For young cadets like Ross, this was an exciting time to join the ranks of military pilots.

Ross underwent rigorous training at Kelly Field in Texas, one of the primary training bases for the Army Air Corps. Kelly Field had a long history of pilot training dating back to the First World War, and it was here that Ross honed his flying skills. The training was physically and mentally demanding, but Ross excelled, earning his pilot's wings on 30 June 1937 and receiving a commission as a second lieutenant.

After his commissioning, Ross was assigned to the 20th Pursuit Group at Barksdale Field in Louisiana. The 20th Pursuit Group was one of the Air Corps' early combat units, and Ross's assignment there was a testament to his skills and potential as a pilot. He flew Curtiss P-6 Hawks and Boeing P-26 Peashooters, two of the primary fighter aircraft of the time. The P-26, in particular, was a significant aircraft in U.S. aviation history as the first all-metal monoplane to enter service with the Army Air Corps.

During this period, aviation technology was advancing rapidly. The biplanes of the First World War were being replaced by more advanced monoplanes, and new innovations in engine design, aerodynamics, and armament were changing the capabilities of military aircraft. Ross was at the forefront of these developments, gaining valuable experience in both flying and maintaining these advanced aircraft.

Shortly after his arrival at Barksdale Field, Ross took leave to marry his college sweetheart, Dorothy Isabel Watson, known as "Dot." Their wedding took place on 11 November 1937 in Olympia, Washington. The couple's marriage was a partnership that endured the many challenges and trials of Ross's military career. Like many military wives of the time, Dorothy played a crucial role in supporting her husband's career, often enduring long periods of separation and the uncertainties of war. The couple had two sons.

After their marriage, Ross and Dorothy faced an early challenge when Dorothy became ill with the flu. The newlyweds embarked on a long and arduous journey from Washington back to Louisiana in Ross's 1935 Plymouth sedan. What should have taken only a few days turned into a three-week ordeal due to car trouble and Dorothy's illness. This experience, described in Ross's book *Not as Briefed*, highlighted the resilience and determination that would characterize their life together.

As tensions escalated in Europe and Asia, the U.S. military began preparing for the possibility of a global war. Ross was then serving as a pilot of both B-18 and B-25 Mitchell aircraft. He also served as the commander of the 19th Air Base Squadron and as provost marshal of the 17th Bomb Group, stationed first at McChord Field, Washington, and later at Pendleton Army Airfield, Oregon. He held these roles from June 1940 until his selection for the Doolittle Raid in February 1942.

Ross was disappointed when he was not initially selected as a volunteer for the mission. At the time, he was on a training flight with Colonel Robert Emmens, who would later become a fellow Doolittle Raider. Upon their return, they discovered that the volunteer slots had already been filled. Their superior, Jack Hilger, recognized their disappointment and suggested that they join the mission as instructors at Eglin Field, Florida, where the crews were being trained for the raid.

Ross and Robert Emmens agreed and joined the group at Eglin Field. During the training, Ross's skills and leadership qualities became evident, and he was eventually selected as a replacement for a pilot who had withdrawn from the mission.

As the ordnance officer for the mission, Ross played a crucial role in addressing the limitations of the bombers' equipment. He realized that the Norden bombsight, a sophisticated but bulky device, was not suitable for the low-level bombing required for the raid and designed a simpler, more effective bombsight. His invention, known as the "Mark Twain" bombsight, was a lightweight, practical tool for conducting precise low-level bombing.

The "Mark Twain" bombsight, named after the way Mississippi River steamboats measured water depth, was far less complex than the Norden bombsight. It consisted of a small square marked in degrees and a sighting post resembling a rifle sight. This design allowed the bombardier to quickly and accurately align the bombsight with the target during low-level bombing runs. The simplicity of the device made it more suited to the type of bombing the Doolittle Raiders would carry out, where speed and adaptability were critical.

The "Mark Twain" bombsight was not only a technical innovation but also a key factor in the success of the Doolittle Raid. Thanks to his ingenuity and problem-solving abilities, Ross helped ensure that the bombers could effectively carry out their mission despite the challenging conditions.

On 18 April 1942, the Doolittle Raiders launched their attack on Japan. Despite the challenges caused by having to start the mission earlier than planned, Ross and the other raiders successfully carried out the bombing raid, striking targets in Tokyo and other cities. Ross flew with Crew 11, and the eleventh plane took off from the USS *Hornet* at 8:56 am. It bore the USAAF serial number 40-2249 and the NAA manufacturer number B62-2918. The aircraft was named "Hari-Kari'er."

As we know, the bombers did not have enough fuel to reach their planned landing sites in China. Ross's plane, like the others, was forced to bail out over China after running out of fuel. Ross and his crew were aided by Chinese villagers, who helped them evade Japanese forces and make their way to Chongqing, the capital of Free China.

After the success of the Doolittle Raid, Ross Greening continued to serve in the U.S. Army Air Forces, rising in rank and taking on new challenges. However, his wartime adventures were far from over. In July 1943, during a mission over Naples, Italy, Ross's plane was shot down by enemy fire. The right engine of his aircraft was hit, and Ross ordered his crew to bail out. During his descent, Ross was injured by a bullet near his knee, dislocated his hip, and sprained both ankles. He narrowly avoided landing in the crater of Mount Vesuvius.

Captured by German and Italian forces, Ross was taken to a prisoner of war camp in Italy. The conditions in the camp were harsh, and the uncertainty of the war's outcome weighed heavily on the prisoners. Despite these hardships, Ross's resilience and leadership shone through in captivity. He worked to boost the morale of his fellow prisoners, organizing activities to keep their spirits high.

In September 1943, after Italy's surrender, the German Army took over the POW camp. Plans were made to transport the prisoners to Germany, but during an air raid on Bolzano, Italy, on 3 October 1943, Ross managed to escape from the prison transport train. His escape marked the beginning of a six-month period in which he eluded capture with the help of compassionate Italians in the areas of Verona and Cividale.

During his time on the run, Ross shared a mountain cave with two New Zealand escapees, Bob Smith and Jack Lang. They received food aid from local villagers, who risked their lives to help the Allied soldiers. The Italian countryside was a dangerous place for escapees, as German patrols were constantly searching for them. Despite the challenges, Ross never lost hope of evading capture.

Ross was recaptured by German forces in March 1944 and sent to Stalag Luft I, a prisoner of war camp for captured Allied airmen, located near Barth, Western Pomerania, Germany. The camp, which housed thousands of airmen from various Allied countries, was known for its harsh conditions and strict discipline. Despite these challenges, Ross once again turned to his artistic talents to pass the time and boost his morale.

At Stalag Luft I, Ross organized drawing classes for his fellow prisoners, teaching them the basics of sketching and painting. He also made portraits, battle scenes as described by other prisoners, and organized weekly art exhibitions in the camp's mess hall. His artistic talents provided a creative outlet for the prisoners and helped foster a sense of community and solidarity.

In addition to his work as an artist, Ross was involved in organizing the "*Kriegie Kraft Karnival*," an event held in the camp from 21 to 23 July 1944, which showcased the artwork and models created by prisoners from across the camp. The event was a testament to the resilience and ingenuity of the prisoners, who found ways to create beauty and meaning even in the most difficult circumstances.

The end of the war in Europe came in May 1945, and with Germany's surrender, the prisoners at Stalag Luft I were liberated by advancing Allied forces. Ross was flown out of the camp on 14 May 1945, along with fifty-six crates of artwork and crafts made by the prisoners. These items were later used to prepare a prisoner of war exhibition, which included a reproduction of the camp's sixteen-man room, a solitary confinement cell, and escape attempts. The exhibition opened on 1 October 1945 at the Rockefeller Center Museum of Science and Industry and later traveled to various U.S. cities before ending in Washington, D.C., in September 1946.

After the war, Ross Greening continued to serve in the U.S. Air Force, which was established as a separate branch of the military in 1947. His post-war career was marked by a series of important assignments that contributed to the strategic capabilities of the Air Force during the early years of the Cold War.

From June 1945 to September 1946, Ross served as the head of the Army Air Forces Prisoner of War Exposition, overseeing the reintegration and support of returning POWs. This role was crucial in the post-war period, as many returning prisoners faced significant challenges in adjusting to civilian life or returning to active duty. Ross's leadership helped address the complex needs of these servicemen and ensured that they received the support and recognition they deserved.

Following this assignment, Ross took on roles focused on the training and development of the next generation of Air Force leaders. From December 1946 to August 1948, he served as director of the syndicate division and later as head of the seminar division at the Air Tactical School at Tyndall Air Force Base in Florida. These roles placed him at the forefront of developing tactical and operational training programs for Air Force officers, ensuring they were well-prepared for the challenges of the emerging Cold War.

Recognizing the importance of continuing education in military leadership, Ross attended the Armed Forces Staff College in Norfolk, Virginia, from August 1948 to January 1949. This period of study provided him with advanced knowledge in joint operations and strategic planning, which he applied in his subsequent assignments.

After completing his studies, Ross was assigned to McGuire Air Force Base in New Jersey, where he served as both an RB-17 Flying Fortress and RB-29 Superfortress pilot and the director of operations and training for the 91st Strategic Reconnaissance Wing. In this role, he played a crucial part in overseeing reconnaissance missions that were vital for gathering intelligence during the early Cold War. His expertise in operations and training was essential in maintaining the readiness and effectiveness of the reconnaissance wing.

In June 1949, Ross was promoted to commander of the 91st Strategic Reconnaissance Group at McGuire AFB, a position he held until August 1949. His leadership during this period further solidified his reputation as a capable commander responsible for one of the most important strategic reconnaissance units within the Air Force.

Ross continued to expand his expertise in strategic planning with his next assignment. From September to October 1949, he attended the U.S. Air Force Special Staff School at Craig Air Force Base in Alabama. This advanced training prepared him for a series of highly specialized roles within the headquarters of the U.S. Air Force at the Pentagon.

From November 1949 to August 1953, Ross held various key positions within the Pentagon. As chief of special projects and staff planning officer in the domestic branch of the policy division, and later as chief of the domestic branch in the policy division, he was involved in high-level strategic planning and policy development. His work during this period was critical in shaping the Air Force's domestic operations and strategic policies during the early years of the Cold War.

In recognition of his outstanding service, Ross was selected to attend the prestigious Air War College at Maxwell Air Force Base in Alabama from August 1953 to August 1954. This senior-level professional military education institution is designed to prepare officers for high command positions and staff responsibilities. His time at the Air War College further sharpened his strategic thinking and leadership skills.

Upon graduating, Ross attended the attaché course at the Strategic Intelligence School in Washington, D.C., from August to November 1954. This course prepared him for a key diplomatic assignment, where his role would extend beyond traditional military duties and involve significant diplomatic responsibilities.

In January 1955, Ross was appointed as air attaché to Australia and New Zealand, a key position in which he served as the senior Air Force representative in these allied nations. His role involved fostering strong military and diplomatic relations, coordinating with allied air forces, and representing the interests of the U.S. Air Force in the region. Ross's leadership and diplomatic skills were crucial in maintaining and strengthening the ties between the United States and its allies in the South Pacific.

Ten years after his release from captivity, Ross and his wife returned to Italy in an attempt to find the Italians who had helped him during his escape in the mountains. The couple successfully located his former friends. The Italian villagers affectionately referred to him as "The Brave Colonel."

Unfortunately, Ross Greening's distinguished career was prematurely cut short by illness. In June 1956, he was forced to return to the United States due to a severe health condition: a blood infection that attacked his heart. Upon his return, he was admitted to Walter Reed Army Hospital where he remained as a patient. Despite the best efforts of medical professionals, Ross's health continued to decline.

His illness was severe and ultimately untreatable by the medical advancements of the time. The condition was serious enough to significantly affect his ability to remain in active service. This period of his life was marked by a gradual decline in his health.

On 29 March 1957, Colonel Charles Ross Greening passed away in the Walter Reed Army Hospital, Washington, while still on active duty. He died from an infection of the lining of the heart. His death marked the loss of a dedicated and highly respected officer who had served his country with distinction for many years. In recognition of his service, Ross was buried with full military honors at Arlington National Cemetery, a tribute to his contributions to the U.S. Air Force and his country.

Colonel Greening's career is a shining example of the dedication, resilience, and adaptability required of military leaders, especially during times of significant global tensions and conflict. His work in strategic reconnaissance, training, and diplomatic service left a lasting impact on the capabilities of the U.S. Air Force and the relationships with key allies. Although his life was cut short, his legacy lives on in the generations of Air Force personnel he trained and the policies he helped shape. His final resting place at Arlington National Cemetery stands as a lasting tribute to a man who devoted his life to the service of his country.

The story of Ross Greening is not just one of personal achievement but also of the broader historical currents that shaped his life and career. His experiences during the Second World War, including his role in the Doolittle Raid and his time as a prisoner of war, reflect the courage and sacrifice of the "Greatest Generation." His post-war career, marked by significant contributions to Cold War military strategy and diplomacy, underscores the importance of leadership and vision in maintaining global peace and security.

Ross's book, *Not as Briefed*, has a fascinating backstory. He had accumulated a considerable collection of war memorabilia, including a diary, logbook, sketches, and letters. Before his death, Ross had tried to organize these materials into a book with the help of a professional author. Unfortunately, both Ross and the author passed away before they could complete the project. Ross had recorded many of his memories on a dictaphone, but the project remained unfinished. The materials were largely forgotten in boxes for about forty years until one evening, Ross's niece, Karen Morgan Driscoll, rediscovered them. She, along with Ross's wife and other family members, took on the task of completing the book, which was eventually published in 2001. The book offers a rich account of wartime memories, includes Ross's sketches, and serves as an engaging source of insight into his life.

When we look back on his life, it is clear that Ross embodied the highest ideals of military service. His dedication to his country, his innovative spirit, and his unwavering commitment to his fellow servicemen continue to inspire. His legacy is one of honor, duty, and service, a legacy that will endure for generations to come.

Colonel Ross Greening was a lover of the arts, and his passion for art played a significant role throughout his life. His studies Washington State College (now Washington State University) included not only traditional artistic techniques but also an exploration of creative expression, which would later become an integral part of his identity, even as he pursued a military career.

Ross's artistic talents were not merely a hobby but a central aspect of his life. His ability to draw and paint provided him with a valuable creative outlet, especially during the more challenging moments of his military career, particularly while held as a prisoner of war during. His art was more than just a personal passion; it became a tool of resilience and a way to boost morale in difficult circumstances. Greening's contributions to the arts, both in and out of uniform, underscore his multifaceted character, one that combined the discipline and determination of a military officer with the sensitivity and creativity of an artist. His legacy as both a pilot and an artist remains an inspiration for those who learn about his life and accomplishments.

Pilot of Crew 12

Colonel William M. Bower

Colonel William Marsh “Bill” Bower was born on 13 February 1917 in Ravenna, Ohio, a small, picturesque town known for its tight-knit community and rich history. He was the only child of Dr Harold Bower and Catharine Marsh. Dr Harold Bower was a respected local physician, widely known in the community for his medical excellence and compassion. His work as a doctor was not just a profession but a calling, deeply rooted in his dedication to helping those in need. He was an authoritative figure, full of kindness, and often went above and beyond to ensure the wellbeing of his patients. This dedication to service greatly influenced young William, instilling in him a strong sense of duty and compassion.

Catharine Marsh, William’s mother, had an equally significant influence on his upbringing. Known for her caring nature and dedication to her family, she created a warm and loving home environment where strong family bonds were cherished and traditional values were passed on to her son. Beyond her role as a homemaker, Catharine was actively involved in community activities, demonstrating the importance of civic duty and community service. Her gentle guidance and supportive nature provided William with a stable and nurturing foundation, essential for his personal development.

Growing up in such a supportive environment, William had a childhood rich in family values and community involvement.

The Bower household was a place of intellectual curiosity and lively discussions. Dr Bower's profession brought a constant flow of medical literature and conversations about the latest advancements in medicine. These discussions were not limited to medicine but often extended to other areas of science and technology, particularly aviation. William, a curious and eager child, was naturally drawn to these conversations surrounding new inventions and discoveries, especially those about flying.

A pivotal moment in William's youth was his introduction to aviation. From a young age, he showed a fascination with airplanes, a passion that was encouraged and supported by his parents. The Bower family nurtured their son's growing interest by providing him with books and materials on aviation. They recognized the potential of this interest and made efforts to introduce William to the world of flight. This included trips to airshows and other aviation-related events, where he could see airplanes up close and learn more about their mechanics and operation. These experiences were crucial in shaping his ambitions and deepening his passion for aviation.

William's formal education began at the local public schools in Ravenna, starting at Chestnut Street School and later at Highland Avenue School. These institutions, typical of small-town America, offered a broad education that emphasized not only academic achievement but also moral development and civic duty. William was an exemplary student, known for his eagerness to learn. He excelled in subjects like science and mathematics, which were not only his favorites but also areas where he showed significant aptitude. His teachers often remarked on his inquisitive nature and his ability to grasp complex concepts, qualities that would serve him well in his later career.

One of the most formative experiences of William's early aviation journey was his first encounter with flying at the age of 9. In 1926, he had the opportunity to fly in a Waco biplane, a popular aircraft of the time known for its sturdy construction and versatility. For young William, the experience of being in the air was exhilarating. The sensation of flight, the sound of the engine, and the feeling of soaring above the ground left a lasting impression on him. This experience was not merely thrilling but a defining moment that cemented his passion for aviation. During that flight, William realized his dream of becoming a pilot, a dream that would guide his future efforts.

Another significant event in William's early life was attending the National Air Races in Cleveland, Ohio, in 1932. At 15, William was determined to attend this major aviation event, which brought together the most advanced aircraft and skilled pilots of the time. The National Air Races were a showcase of the latest aviation technology and aerial acrobatics, attracting thousands of spectators from across the country. William, as determined as ever, saved enough money for a train ticket and hitchhiked to the airfield. There, he watched in awe as pilots performed daring maneuvers and competed in various races. One of the highlights of the event was James Doolittle's victory in the Thompson Trophy Race, flying the Gee Bee R-1 Super Sportster. The Gee Bee R-1 was an engineering marvel, known for its speed and agility. Doolittle's skillful handling of the aircraft and his triumph in the race left a lasting impression on William. This experience further fueled his passion for aviation and strengthened his resolve to pursue a career as a pilot.

In 1934, William graduated from Ravenna High School. During his high school years, he was actively involved in various school activities. He was a member of the debate team, where he honed his public speaking and analytical skills. He also participated in sports, showcasing his versatility and athletic ability. These extracurricular activities provided him with a well-rounded education, teaching him the importance of teamwork, discipline, and perseverance. It was also during this period that William's interest in aviation grew significantly. The stories of early aviation pioneers like Charles Lindbergh and

Amelia Earhart greatly influenced him. The accomplishments of these pilots, who pushed the boundaries of what was possible, fascinated William and fueled his desire to explore the skies.

After high school, William continued his education at Hiram College, a small liberal arts college in Ohio. His time at Hiram College was marked by intellectual exploration and academic growth. William was interested in the sciences, particularly aviation and technology. He pursued a curriculum that included subjects such as physics, chemistry, and mathematics, laying a strong foundation for his future studies and career. In addition to his academic pursuits, William was a member of the university's aviation club, where he had the opportunity to engage with like-minded individuals and further explore his passion for flying.

In 1936, William transferred to Kent State University, where he continued his studies. This period was one of personal growth and exploration. While at Kent State, William expanded his knowledge and skills in various fields, including engineering and aeronautics. He took advantage of the university's resources to deepen his understanding of aircraft mechanics and flight theory. However, his time at Kent State was relatively short, as he decided to leave the university to pursue a more direct path into aviation. This decision was driven by his unwavering passion for flying and his desire to join the growing field of military aviation. William often referred to this decision as earning his "Highway 66 diploma," a nod to his adventurous spirit and the iconic Route 66, symbolizing his journey westward in search of opportunities in aviation.

In 1936, William took a significant step toward his dream of becoming a pilot by joining the Ohio National Guard. He enlisted in the 107th Cavalry, a unit with a rich history and tradition. His decision to join the National Guard was motivated by his desire to serve his country and gain valuable military experience. The 107th Cavalry, based in Ravenna, Ohio, provided William with his first exposure to military life. The training was rigorous and comprehensive, covering a wide range of military skills. William learned everything from cavalry tactics to basic soldiering skills, acquiring the discipline and knowledge necessary for a military career.

During his time in the National Guard, William maintained a strong interest in aviation. Although the 107th Cavalry was not an aviation unit, William sought opportunities to learn more about aircraft and flying. He participated in any available training related to aviation and studied aircraft mechanics in his spare time. His dedication to learning and his passion for flying did not go unnoticed. William's superiors recognized his potential and supported his ambitions to transition to a role where he could more directly pursue his passion for aviation.

In 1939, as the world stood on the brink of war, William took further steps to immerse himself in aviation. Although formal records of his military aviation training during this period are limited, it is likely that he pursued additional training through private or civilian channels. William may have taken flying lessons at a local airfield or participated in civilian aviation programs to gain flight experience. This preparatory period was crucial, as it gave him the skills and knowledge needed to qualify for formal military flight training. It was also a time of personal growth, as William developed a deeper understanding of the complexities of flying and aviation technology.

On 4 October 1940, William officially joined the United States Army Air Corps, marking the beginning of a distinguished military career. He enlisted at Fort Hayes in Columbus, Ohio, and was subsequently admitted to the prestigious Aviation Cadet Training Program at Randolph Field, Texas. Known as the "West Point of the Air," Randolph Field was a premier training facility for aspiring military pilots. The program was designed to produce highly skilled pilots capable of flying the most advanced aircraft and handling the rigors of combat. As a newly commissioned officer, William was assigned to the 37th Bomb Squadron at Lowry Field in Denver, Colorado. The 37th Bomb Squadron was part of the 17th Bombardment Group, a unit that would play a critical role in the early stages of the Second World War.

The training at Randolph Field was intense and demanding. It included both classroom instruction and hands-on flight training, covering a wide range of subjects. Cadets received instruction in navigation, meteorology, aircraft mechanics, and combat tactics. They also underwent extensive physical training to prepare them for the physical demands of flying and combat. William excelled in all aspects of the training program. His natural aptitude for flying, combined with his dedication and hard work, set him apart from his peers. He demonstrated exceptional skill in both the theoretical and practical aspects of aviation, earning high marks in all his courses.

At Lowry Field, William began his training with the B-18 Bolo bomber. The B-18 was a twin-engine bomber that had been in service since the mid-1930s. It was a reliable aircraft, but its design was considered obsolete compared to newer models. Nevertheless, the B-18 provided valuable training experience for William and his fellow pilots. They conducted numerous training missions, honing their skills in navigation, bombing, and formation flying.

In 1940–41, the 17th Bomb Group underwent a major transition, with the B-18 Bolo being replaced by the more advanced B-25 Mitchell bomber. The transition to the B-25 required extensive training and adaptation, as the new aircraft had different flight characteristics and operational capabilities. William and his fellow pilots spent months familiarizing themselves with the B-25, learning to handle the aircraft's advanced avionics and weaponry.

In June 1941, William and the 17th Bombardment Group were transferred to McChord Field in Washington. McChord Field was one of the first Army Air Corps bases to receive the B-25 Mitchell, and it became a key training center for the new bomber. The training program at McChord Field was intensive, designed to prepare the crews for various combat scenarios. The pilots and crews practiced long-range navigation, formation flying, and precision bombing, all essential skills for the upcoming conflict. William quickly adapted to the new aircraft and excelled in his training, further establishing himself as a skilled and capable bomber pilot.

In early 1942, with the United States fully engaged in the Second World War, William volunteered for the top-secret mission that would later become known as the Doolittle Raid.

Following extensive training at Eglin Field, Florida, William was selected to lead the crew of the 12th B-25, initially named "Werewolf." However, due to an accident while loading the plane in Alameda, California, the plane's name was changed to "Fickle Finger of Fate." Despite the name change, William and his crew remained focused on the mission.

The task force, consisting of the aircraft carriers USS *Hornet* and USS *Enterprise*, along with fourteen support ships, departed from San Francisco on 2 April 1942. On 18 April 1942, all sixteen planes successfully launched from *Hornet*, with William's plane taking off at 8:59 am as the twelfth airplane. The bombers flew at low altitude to avoid detection and navigated to their targets using a combination of dead reckoning and celestial navigation. William piloted the B-25 bomber with the factory serial number 62B-2947 and USAAF serial number 40-2278, named "Fickle Finger of Fate."

William's plane, like the others, faced formidable challenges as it approached Japan. The planes encountered anti-aircraft fire and enemy fighters as they neared their targets. Despite these dangers, William and his crew successfully bombed their assigned targets in Yokohama, including shipyards and an oil refinery. The mission's objectives were achieved, and damage was inflicted on Japan's industrial and military infrastructure. However, the attack was only half of the mission; the crews still had to escape.

The original plan had been for the bombers to fly to China, where they would land at a prearranged airfield. However, due to the early launch, the planes had less fuel than anticipated and as the bombers neared the Chinese coast, they encountered severe weather and headwinds, further depleting their fuel reserves. The crews realized they could not reach the designated airfield and would have to either bail out or crash-land in China.

William and his crew parachuted from their plane over China. As they landed in unfamiliar territory, they faced the daunting challenge of evading Japanese forces and finding safety. William landed safely and, with the help of local Chinese villagers, found his way to safety. On the ground, Crew 12 joined four members of Crew 10. The villagers, who risked their own lives, provided shelter to the American crew members and helped them avoid Japanese patrols. William's experience in China was a harrowing ordeal, but it was also a testament to the bravery and generosity of the Chinese people who aided the Doolittle Raiders.

After the Doolittle Raid, William returned to the United States, where he and the other surviving raiders were celebrated as heroes. Upon his return, William participated in war bond tours, using his new-found fame to promote the war effort and raise funds for the military. He also continued his military service, taking on new assignments and responsibilities. In July 1942, he was deployed to England as part of the 12th Air Force, where he served until January 1943. During this time, he was involved in planning and coordinating air operations, contributing to the Allied efforts in Europe.

In early 1943, William was deployed to North Africa, where he served as a B-25 pilot and assistant operations officer for the 47th Bomb Wing. His role included planning and executing bombing missions, as well as overseeing the wing's squadron operations. From May 1943 to September 1944, he served as operations officer for the 310th Bomb Group, a unit that played a critical role in the

Mediterranean theater. The 310th Bomb Group conducted numerous missions over North Africa, Italy, and southern Europe, targeting enemy installations, transportation networks, and military formations.

William's leadership and expertise were instrumental in the success of these missions. He was responsible for coordinating the group's operations and ensuring that the missions were carried out effectively and efficiently. His ability to plan and execute complex operations earned him the respect of his peers and superiors. In September 1944, he was appointed as operations officer for the 57th Bomb Wing in Italy, where he continued to play a key role in the Allied air campaign.

In July 1945, William assumed command of the 310th Bomb Group in Italy. As commander, he oversaw the group's transition from combat operations to post-war activities. Under his leadership, the group continued to carry out missions until the end of the war in Europe.

After the Second World War, William continued his military career in the United States Air Force (USAF), which became a separate branch of the U.S. military in 1947. From July to December 1948, he attended the Air Command and Staff College at Maxwell AFB, Alabama, further enhancing his leadership and strategic planning skills. His education at the Air Command and Staff College prepared him for higher command positions and staff roles, giving him the knowledge and skills needed to manage the complexities of post-war military operations.

After graduating, William served as senior air instructor with the Colorado Air National Guard at Lowry AFB from December 1948 to February 1949. In this role, he was responsible for training and mentoring National Guard pilots, sharing his extensive experience and expertise. His contributions were invaluable in helping build a strong and capable National Guard force.

In February 1949, William was assigned to the headquarters of the U.S. Air Force at the Pentagon, where he served until November 1952.

During this time, he worked in various roles, contributing to the development of Air Force policy and programs. He played a key role in planning and implementing initiatives aimed at modernizing the Air Force and expanding its capabilities.

From December 1952 to May 1953, he served as chief of programs, plans, and requirements on the staff of the Northeast Air Command at Pepperrell AFB, Newfoundland, Canada. In this role, he was responsible for overseeing the planning and execution of air operations in the northeastern part of the Atlantic. He also commanded the 6622nd Air Transport Squadron and later the 6614th Air Transport Group, overseeing critical air transport operations from May 1953 to November 1955.

William's career continued to flourish as he took on increasingly responsible positions. From December 1955 to October 1958, he served on the staff of the 1002nd Inspector General Group at Norton AFB, California. He then became the base commander of the 2589th Air Base Group at Dobbins AFB, Georgia, a position he held from November 1958 to July 1960. In this role, he was responsible for overseeing the base's operations and ensuring its readiness for various missions.

In July 1960, William assumed the role of liaison officer for the Rocky Mountain Region of the Civil Air Patrol at Lowry AFB, Colorado. He served in this capacity until August 1964, maintaining relations between the Air Force and the Civil Air Patrol and supporting various community-based aviation activities. His final assignment was as director of logistics for the 26th Air Division and 1st Air Force at Stewart AFB, New York, from August 1964 to April 1966. He concluded his distinguished military career as head of the overseas logistics department for the 1st Air Force at Stewart AFB, retiring on 1 September 1966.

After retiring from the Air Force, Colonel William Marsh Bower settled in Boulder, Colorado, where he became an active member of the local community. He and his family moved to a home on Dennison Lane, where they lived for many years. In Boulder, Colonel Bower quickly became a respected figure, known for his dedication to public service and community involvement.

Colonel Bower's post-retirement activities were diverse and impactful. He was involved in several civic organizations and played a key role in community development. He was instrumental in founding the local chapter of the Air Force Association and held the honorary title of flight captain with the Order of Daedalians, an organization of military pilots. He also served on the board of directors for Crime Stoppers and the Retired Seniors Volunteer Program, contributing his time and expertise to these important initiatives.

In Boulder, William was actively involved in local government and environmental issues. He served on various city commissions, including those overseeing aviation noise and operations, as well as the Boulder Creek Flood Control. His contributions to these commissions were invaluable, helping address important community concerns and improving the quality of life for Boulder residents. Additionally, he worked for ten years on the commission of U.S. Congressman Tom Wirth, screening candidates for the nation's service academies, helping to select and mentor the next generation of military leaders.

William was fondly remembered by his neighbors as a "surrogate grandfather, handyman, and caretaker." He was known for his generosity and willingness to help others. Whether it was shoveling sidewalks in the winter or building model rockets for neighborhood children, William was always ready to lend a hand. He had a reputation for being kind and approachable, often handing out Jolly Rancher candies to the kids who visited his home.

An avid outdoorsman, he enjoyed fishing, hunting, and other outdoor activities. He regularly fished on the Rio Grande and enjoyed bird hunting in the mountains of Colorado. In his youth, he was also an accomplished equestrian and introduced his daughters to horseback riding, sharing his love for the activity with them. His passion for the outdoors was a significant part of his life, giving him a deep appreciation for nature and the environment.

Throughout his retirement, Wiliam remained close to his fellow Doolittle Raiders. He actively participated in the raiders' annual reunions, which had been held every year since 1947, except in 1955 and 1966. These reunions were an opportunity for the surviving members of the raid to come together, share stories, and remember their experiences. In 1993, William had the honor of playing "Taps" at the memorial service for James Doolittle, a poignant moment that underscored the deep bonds formed during the raid.

In 2008, Colonel Bower was recognized for his distinguished service during the Memorial Day race in Boulder, an event that honored veterans and celebrated their contributions. His life was a testament to the values of service, dedication, and community. He was a beloved figure in Boulder, remembered not only for his military accomplishments but also for his kindness and generosity.

Colonel William Marsh Bower passed away on 10 January 2011 in Boulder, Colorado, due to complications from a fall he had suffered in July 2009. His death marked the passing of a remarkable individual who had led a life of service and dedication. After his death, he was remembered by many as a hero, a mentor, and a friend. His contributions to his country and community left a lasting legacy, and he continues to be remembered and honored for his remarkable life and career. Colonel Bower was buried with full military honors, a fitting tribute to his distinguished service and dedication.

Colonel William Marsh Bower was buried at Greenwood Memory Lawn Cemetery in Phoenix, Arizona. This location was chosen as his final resting place, where family, friends, and those who admired his service can pay their respects. His grave is a place of honor, reflecting his dedication and the impact he had throughout his life and military career. William was laid to rest in a dignified ceremony, reflecting the respect and admiration he had earned during his life. His grave, marked with a headstone commemorating his service and contributions, serves as a lasting tribute to a man who devoted his life to his country. It stands as a place of remembrance for family, friends, and those who wish to honor the legacy of a true American hero.

Colonel Bower's life was characterized by a deep sense of duty, both in his military service and in his community involvement. His contributions to his country, particularly during the Doolittle Raid, were an important part of American military history. However, his legacy extended beyond his military achievements. He was a devoted family man, a committed public servant, and a valued member of his community. His story is a testament to the impact one person can have through a life of service and dedication.

Pilot of Crew 13

Lieutenant Colonel Edgar E. McElroy

Lieutenant Colonel Edgar Earl "Mac" McElroy was born on 24 March 1912 in the small town of Ennis, Texas. Located in Ellis County, about 35 miles south of Dallas, Ennis was a typical small American town where everyone knew each other, and community values were strong. Edgar was born into a family deeply rooted in these values, where hard work, perseverance, and a sense of duty were instilled from an early age. Ennis was first established in 1871 with the arrival of the Houston and Texas Central Railway, and the community was named after early railway official Colonel Cornelius Ennis.

Edgar's father, Harry McCutcheon McElroy, was a skilled mechanic and owner of an auto repair shop in the heart of the town, close to the fire station. Harry's workshop was a bustling center in the community, a place where the townspeople brought their vehicles for repairs and maintenance. The skills Harry possessed were both practical and invaluable in a time when cars were still considered a luxury by many. Harry's work was not only a means of supporting his family but also a demonstration of the precision and dedication he would pass on to his children.

Edgar's mother, Jennie M. Schmidt, was a descendant of German immigrants. Her heritage brought with it a strong work ethic and a respect for discipline and precision, qualities she instilled in her children. The McElroy household was one where thrift, hard work, and family cohesion were paramount. Jennie was not only a homemaker but also played an important role in ensuring her children received a solid upbringing, infused with both moral and ethical values.

Edgar was the youngest of five children, with one sister and three brothers. Growing up in a large family had its own dynamics: there was always someone to play with, but as the youngest, Edgar also had to find his own space amid the busyness of a bustling household. His siblings often described him as the quiet, introspective, and thoughtful one, always absorbed in his own projects. Unlike his louder siblings, Edgar found solace in solitude, where he could immerse himself in his thoughts and dreams.

The McElroy family lived at 609 North Dallas Street, a modest house that reflected the family's working-class roots. The house was not just a dwelling but a haven of love and warmth. The family was devout and regularly attended the local Presbyterian church. Sunday was not only a day of rest but also a time for family gatherings, where the values of faith and community were reinforced. The church played a significant role in shaping Edgar's worldview in his early years, teaching him the importance of integrity, responsibility, and service to others.

As a child, Edgar was expected to help out in his father's garage after school and on weekends. This was not uncommon for children at the time; work was seen as a part of life, and learning a trade was just as important as formal schooling. Edgar quickly became fascinated by the mechanical world, the workings of engines, the smell of oil, and the satisfaction of fixing something with his own hands. The garage became his playground, a place where he could experiment, learn, and develop skills that would serve him well in the future.

Despite the demands of work, Edgar found time to enjoy the simple pleasures of childhood. He was particularly fascinated by the airplanes that occasionally flew overhead. At a time when aviation was still in its infancy, seeing a plane soar through the sky was a marvel. Edgar would often run into the street to catch a glimpse of these flying machines, squinting against the sun as he watched them disappear into the horizon. In those moments, a dream was born, a dream that one day, he would be up there, among the clouds, piloting one of those magnificent machines.

Edgar's early love for machines wasn't limited to airplanes. He was also passionate about cars. By the time he was a teenager, he had decided to build his own Model-T from spare parts. It was a project that consumed him, requiring him to gather parts from various vehicles: a frame from one place, an engine from another, wheels from yet another. The car, when it was finally assembled, was far from beautiful, but it was functional, and most importantly, it was his own creation. Edgar was immensely proud as he drove his homemade car down the dusty roads of Ennis, experiencing the thrill of freedom and speed. His car, though rudimentary, could reach speeds of up to 40 miles per hour, a significant achievement for a young man with limited resources.

There is little documentation about Edgar's specific experiences in elementary school or even the name of the school he attended. Given the small-town setting of Ennis, it is likely that he attended a local school where practical education was central. In those days, schools in rural Texas focused on providing students with the basic skills needed for daily life, such as reading, writing, and arithmetic, while also instilling a sense of community and responsibility.

Edgar spent his high school years at Ennis High School, which he attended from approximately 1926 to 1930. These were formative years for him, during which his interest in mechanics and aviation became more than just a hobby. High school gave Edgar the opportunity to further develop his passions, and he quickly became known for his mechanical abilities. Whether it was fixing a classmate's car or building a model airplane, Edgar's talents were evident to everyone who knew him.

In addition to his academic pursuits, Edgar was also an athlete. He played both football and tennis, excelling particularly in football, where his skills on the field earned him an athletic scholarship to Trinity University in Waxahachie. This scholarship was not only a recognition of his athletic abilities but also an opportunity for him to further his education, something highly valued in the McElroy household. Despite his success in sports, Edgar's true passion lay elsewhere. He often admitted that he daydreamed in class, his thoughts drifting away from the subject at hand to the clouds, where he imagined himself as the pilot of his own airplane.

During high school, Edgar took an important step toward his dream of becoming a pilot. He enrolled in a correspondence course in aircraft mechanics, a decision that would lay the foundation for his future career in aviation. The course gave him a greater understanding of how airplanes worked and complemented the mechanical skills he had already developed in his father's garage.

After high school, Edgar continued his education at Texas Technological College (now Texas Tech University), where he earned a degree in electrical engineering. College was a time of both academic and personal growth for Edgar. He excelled in his studies, demonstrating a keen understanding of complex technical concepts. His professors recognized his potential and often praised his ability to grasp difficult subjects and apply them practically.

During his time at Texas Tech, Edgar was also involved in various extracurricular activities, although his primary focus remained on his studies and his dream of flying. He graduated in 1938 with a degree in electrical engineering, a significant achievement that opened doors to various career opportunities. Despite the promising prospects in the engineering field, Edgar could not shake his desire to fly.

After graduation, Edgar returned to his hometown of Ennis, where he ran a gas station with his brother. This was a time of great economic hardship, as the United States was still recovering from the Great

Depression. The economic situation made it difficult to find stable work, and many young men, including Edgar, had to take whatever opportunities they could to make a living and support their families. The gas station was not a great success, but it provided Edgar with a way to stay connected with his community and earn some money.

In addition to running the gas station, Edgar took on several other jobs to make ends meet. He drove a bus, which allowed him to generate some extra income, and he also worked as a machinist in Longview, Texas. These jobs were far from what he had envisioned for himself, but they gave him valuable work experience and a steady income at a time when that was not guaranteed. The hard work and long days Edgar put in not only helped him support his family but also kept his dream of becoming a pilot alive.

Despite the tough circumstances, Edgar never lost his determination. He continued to believe that one day he would have the opportunity to pursue his passion for aviation. The skills he developed during this period, such as perseverance, responsibility, and hard work, would later prove invaluable during his military career. It was this time of personal sacrifice and hardship that shaped Edgar and prepared him for the challenges he would later face as a pilot and officer in the Army Air Corps.

With the little money he managed to save through these various jobs, Edgar was eventually able to pursue his dream. His determination and hard work ultimately led him to enroll in the Army Air Corps' Flying Cadet Program, marking the beginning of a long and successful military career.

On 23 January 1937, Edgar married Agnes Glenn "Aggie" Gill in Gregg, Texas. Agnes was born on 13 January 1916 in Grand Cane, De Soto, Louisiana. She was a woman of strong character, with a deep sense of family and a supportive nature that would prove invaluable to Edgar throughout his life. The couple had two sons, and their marriage was a partnership in every sense. Agnes provided the emotional support that allowed Edgar to pursue his dreams, while Edgar worked hard to provide for his family.

The early years of their marriage were marked by the same challenges faced by many young couples during the Great Depression: uncertainty, financial difficulties, and the need to make sacrifices. However, Edgar and Agnes faced these challenges together, drawing strength from each other and from their shared values. Their relationship was built on mutual respect, love, and a deep-rooted commitment to their family.

As Edgar's career began to take shape, Agnes played a crucial role in managing the household and raising their children. She was the backbone of the family, ensuring that their sons were well cared for and that the household ran smoothly, even during times of stress and uncertainty. Agnes understood the demands of Edgar's career and the sacrifices it required, and she supported him unconditionally, even when this meant long periods of separation or the uncertainty that came with a military life.

For Edgar, his family was his anchor. No matter where his career took him, whether it was a remote training base, a combat mission, or a far-off post, he always knew he had a home to return to, a place where he was loved and supported. This sense of stability and connection was crucial to him, giving him the strength and courage to face the many challenges ahead.

In November 1940, as the world stood on the brink of war, Edgar decided to enlist in the United States Army Air Corps. This decision was not made lightly; it was the result of years of dreaming, planning, and preparing. By this time, Edgar was 28 years old, older than many of the young men who were enlisting. However, he brought with him a wealth of experience, both in terms of his mechanical skills and his education in electrical engineering.

After enlisting, Edgar underwent intensive pilot training, consisting of both ground school and flight training. Ground school was an intensive program in which Edgar and his fellow students learned the technical aspects of flying, including navigation, meteorology, aircraft mechanics, and flight theory. The curriculum was demanding and required a strong understanding of both the theoretical and practical aspects of aviation.

Flight training was where Edgar truly excelled. His early experiences in his father's garage, combined with his formal education, gave him a unique advantage. He understood the mechanics of the aircraft better than many of his peers and had a natural feel for flying. His instructors quickly recognized his potential, and Edgar soon found himself at the top of his class.

On 12 July 1941, after months of rigorous training, Edgar was commissioned as a lieutenant and received his pilot's wings at Stockton Field, California. It was a moment of immense pride for Edgar, the culmination of years of hard work and dedication. His first assignment was as a B-25 Mitchell pilot with the 37th Bomb Squadron of the 17th Bombardment Group at Pendleton Field, Oregon. Edgar quickly became proficient in flying the B-25, mastering the nuances of the aircraft and earning a reputation as a skilled and reliable pilot. His time with the 17th Bombardment Group was crucial in preparing him for the challenges ahead.

In February 1942, just two months after the United States entered the Second World War following the attack on Pearl Harbor, Edgar volunteered for the Doolittle Raid. Selection for the Doolittle Raid was rigorous. Volunteers were chosen based on their flying experience, their proficiency with the B-25 Mitchell bomber, and their ability to operate under extreme conditions. Edgar's background as an experienced pilot made him a logical choice for the mission.

During their training at Eglin Field in Florida, the volunteers began to understand the significance of the mission, despite the secrecy surrounding the details. In hindsight, they realized that this was not just a bombing raid; it was a symbolic attack on the heart of the Japanese empire, a demonstration that the United States would not be deterred by the attack on Pearl Harbor.

Edgar was assigned to fly the thirteenth aircraft, which took off at 9:01 am on 18 April 1942 from the USS *Hornet*. The B-25 Mitchell, named "Avenger," was known for its reliability, but the crew also knew the mission carried great risk. The aircraft bore the USAAF serial number 40-2247 and the NAA factory number 62B-2916.

Edgar and his crew successfully completed their mission of bombing a target in Japan. They then faced a perilous flight to China, where they were eventually forced to abandon their aircraft due to a fuel shortage. They parachuted into the dark night over China, uncertain of what awaited them on the ground. Fortunately, they were rescued by local Chinese villagers and Catholic missions, who helped them make their way to safety. Edgar later described this experience as one of the most intense moments of his military career.

Edgar subsequently volunteered to fly into Henyan to rescue Dr White (Crew 15) and the seriously wounded Ted Lawson (Crew 7). It was a courageous decision that saw him landing his aircraft on a bomb-damaged runway while the threat of Japanese air attacks loomed overhead. For this act of bravery, he was awarded the Silver Star, one of the highest American military honors.

After the Doolittle Raid, Edgar continued serving in the China-Burma-India theater, starting as a ferry pilot with the Trans-India Ferry Command from May to September 1942. He was then assigned as a B-25 pilot with the 22nd Bomb Squadron of the 341st Bomb Group in India from September 1942 to March 1943. Following this, he was treated for a heart condition at hospitals in India, California, and Texas from March to October 1943. Edgar next served as assistant operations officer with the 47th Bomb Squadron at Randolph Field, Texas, from October to December 1943. He then completed B-24 Liberator transition training from December 1943 to February 1944 and was subsequently appointed as a B-24 instructor pilot and commandant of students at Smyrna, Tennessee, from February to May 1944. Afterward, he served as a B-29 Superfortress pilot with the 24th Bomb Squadron of the 6th Bomb Group at Grand Island Army Airfield, Nebraska, from May to November 1944.

In December 1944, he deployed with the 24th Bomb Squadron to North Field on Tinian in the Mariana Islands, where he flew B-29 combat missions against Japan until March 1945. Edgar was then treated at hospitals in Colorado and California from March to October 1945. He returned to service as assistant adjutant and later as squadron commander of the 2518th Base Unit at Enid, Oklahoma, from October 1945 to May 1946. He briefly commanded the training school at Boca Raton Army Airfield, Florida, from May to June 1946, followed by treatment at Walter Reed General Hospital in Washington, D.C., from June to July 1946.

Next, Edgar served as assistant director of supply and maintenance and later as base shops officer with the 2518th Base Unit at Enid from July to December 1946. From December 1946 to January 1947, he was aircraft maintenance officer with Squadron A at Williams Field, Arizona. He then served as a flight instructor with the 2532nd Base Unit at Randolph Field, Texas, from January to July 1947. Following this, he became a B-29 pilot and assistant A-3 officer with the 718th Bomb Squadron of the 28th Bomb Group at Rapid City Army Airfield, South Dakota, from July 1947 to April 1949.

In April 1949, Edgar took on the role of base operations officer with the 28th Air Base Group at Rapid City AFB, where he served until September 1949. He then moved to Headquarters Strategic Air Command at Offutt AFB, Nebraska, where he served as operations staff officer and later as chief of the flight operations branch from September 1949 to September 1953. His next assignment was as base operations officer and later commander of the 93rd Operations Squadron at Castle AFB, California, from September 1953 to

April 1954. He then served as chief of light bomber operations with the combat operations division at Headquarters Fifth Air Force in Japan from April 1954 to February 1955.

From February to October 1955, he was an operations staff officer with the 1007th Air Intelligence Service Group at the Pentagon, followed by his role as inspector of operations and plans in the operations branch at Andrews AFB, Maryland, from October 1955 to June 1959. He then served as deputy commander of the 1st Aeromedical Transport Group at Brooks AFB, Texas, from June 1959 to May 1960. His next position was as commander of the Operations Squadron with the 6041st Air Base Group at Yokota AB, Japan, from May to December 1960. McElroy's final military assignment was as executive officer with the 6102nd Air Base Group at Yokota AB, a role he held from December 1960 until his retirement on 1 July 1962.

Edgar McElroy passed away on 4 April 2003, and was laid to rest with military honors at Dallas-Fort Worth National Cemetery in Dallas, Texas.

Edgar McElroy left behind a legacy of courage, integrity, and service, reflecting his role as a member of the Doolittle Raiders and his many contributions to the United States Air Force. His life and work remain a testament to duty and determination in the service of his country.

Pilot of Crew 14

Brigadier General John A. Hilger

Brigadier General John Allen "Jack" Hilger was born on 11 January 1909 in Sherman, Texas, a town rich in history and deeply rooted in American tradition. Located in Grayson County, Sherman was a typical small American town of the early twentieth century, characterized by a close-knit community and a rural lifestyle. The German-American heritage of the Hilger family played an important role in shaping the values passed down from generation to generation. German immigrants in the United States were often known for their strong work ethic, discipline, and dedication to family, traits that became characteristic of John and his brothers.

Sherman, like many towns in the United States during this period, was greatly influenced by the far-reaching effects of national and global events. The beginning of the twentieth century was marked by rapid industrialization, the rise of new technologies, and the far-reaching consequences of the First World War. For the Hilger family, these profound changes formed the backdrop of their daily lives. John's father, John Frederick Hilger, worked hard to provide for his family in these tumultuous times, while his mother, Emma Dye, ensured that her children learned the importancc of cducation and moral integrity.

Growing up in Sherman, young John was acutely aware of the challenges his family faced. The First World War left an indelible mark on the local community, with many men going off to fight and returning with stories of the front lines. These stories, told in homes and around the town, were formative for Hilger. They likely sparked a deep sense of patriotism and duty in him, laying the foundation for what would later become a distinguished military career.

As he grew older, the values instilled in him by his parents and community shaped his worldview. Sherman was not a wealthy town, but it was a place where community members supported one another, and integrity was prized above material wealth. Hilger's family, particularly his father, believed in the importance of giving back to the community. As a young man, John often participated in local events, helped his neighbors, and took on responsibilities at home. These formative years were essential in shaping his understanding of duty, a theme that would resonate throughout his military career.

In 1926, after graduating from Sherman High School, John A. Hilger took a major step toward fulfilling his dreams by enrolling at the Agricultural and Mechanical College of Texas (now Texas A&M University). This institution was known for its rigorous academic programs and strong emphasis on military training. For John, Texas A&M was the perfect environment to pursue his interest in mechanical engineering while simultaneously preparing for a military career.

The Corps of Cadets at Texas A&M, a military organization on campus, played a crucial role in John's development. The Corps instilled in its members a deep sense of discipline, duty, and leadership, and John's involvement in the Corps was a transformative experience that provided him with the military training and leadership skills that would later define his career. The Corps also fostered a strong sense of camaraderie among the members, creating bonds that would last a lifetime.

As a student of mechanical engineering, John had a demanding academic schedule, including subjects such as mathematics, physics, thermodynamics, and materials science. The engineering program at Texas A&M was known for its rigor, and John's success in this field demonstrated his intellectual abilities and dedication to his studies. In addition to his academic work, Hilger gained practical experience through hands-on training, which was essential for understanding the complexities of mechanical systems.

However, his time at the university was not without challenges. The onset of the Great Depression in 1929 brought financial difficulties, forcing him to temporarily interrupt his studies. This setback was a major test of John's resilience and determination. Despite the hardships, he remained committed to his education and returned to Texas A&M in the fall of 1931 to complete his degree.

During this period, John also underwent significant personal changes. On 1 March 1931, he married Ina Mae in Atoka, Oklahoma. The couple did not have children, but Ina Mae's support allowed John to fully focus on his career and academic pursuits.

John's perseverance paid off when he graduated from Texas A&M in 1932 with a Bachelor of Science in mechanical engineering. His academic achievements were recognized by his membership in the American Society of Mechanical Engineers, a prestigious professional organization that underscored his dedication to the field of engineering.

After graduation, John was commissioned as a lieutenant in the U.S. Army Reserve through the Army ROTC program. His first commission was in the infantry, reflecting the broad range of training provided by the ROTC program. However, his passion for aviation soon led to a significant career change. On 21 February 1933, he resigned from the infantry to join the Army Air Corps as a flying cadet.

John's transition to the Army Air Corps marked the beginning of a distinguished career in military aviation. His training as a flying cadet took place at Randolph Field, Texas, one of the primary training bases for the U.S. Army Air Corps. Known as the "West Point of the Air," Randolph Field was established to provide comprehensive training for future military pilots.

The Flying Cadet Program at Randolph Field was rigorous, combining academic subjects with practical flight training. Cadets learned various aspects of aviation, including meteorology, navigation, aircraft mechanics, and aerodynamics. The program was designed to produce highly trained pilots capable of meeting the challenges of military aviation.

The training was divided into several phases, with each phase focusing on a different aspect of aviation. The first phase, known as ground school, provided cadets with a solid theoretical foundation. John and his fellow cadets learned about the principles of flight, weather conditions, and the mechanical systems of aircraft. This knowledge was essential for understanding the complexities of operating an aircraft and making informed decisions during flight.

After ground school, the cadets progressed to primary flight training, where they learned basic flight maneuvers, takeoffs, and landings. This phase involved flying with experienced instructors and gradually building confidence in piloting aircraft. Hilger excelled in this phase, demonstrating a natural talent for flying and a keen understanding of the mechanics involved.

As John advanced through the training program, he moved on to more advanced phases, including formation flying, aerial gunnery, and combat tactics. These advanced skills were crucial in preparing cadets for the demands of military aviation, where precision, coordination, and quick decision-making were essential. His success in the Flying Cadet Program earned him his pilot's wings in February

1934, followed by his commission as a lieutenant in the Army Air Corps on 21 February 1935.

John's first assignment as an officer was at March Field, California, a major air base for the Army Air Corps. March Field served as a training and operational center, and his time there provided him with a wide range of experiences. He served in various roles, including pilot, assistant base adjutant, and commanding officer of the base's photographic section.

March Field was a bustling center of activity, with numerous aircraft and personnel engaged in training and operations. John's responsibilities included flight operations, where he gained experience flying various types of aircraft, including the B-18 Bolo, B-23 Dragon, and B-25 Mitchell bombers. These experiences were crucial in developing his flying skills and understanding the capabilities and limitations of different aircraft.

During his time at March Field, John's personal life also underwent significant changes. In March 1937, he and Ina Mae divorced and shortly afterward, on 15 March 1937, he married Virginia Hope Botterud in Los Angeles. The marriage to Virginia brought stability to John's personal life and gave him a supportive partner who understood the demands of a military career. The couple had two children.

In addition to his flying responsibilities, John also took on administrative roles that gave him a broad understanding of base operations. As assistant base adjutant, he was involved in the day-to-day management of the base, including personnel matters and logistical planning. His role as commanding officer of the base's photographic section also gave him insight into the importance of aerial reconnaissance and the use of photography in military operations.

As the 1930s came to a close, the world stood on the brink of a new major conflict. The growing tensions in Europe and Asia foreshadowed the imminent outbreak of the Second World War.

While initially neutral, the United States began preparing for the possibility of involvement in the conflict.

During this period, John continued to develop his skills and gain valuable experience in various assignments. His career advanced as he took on leadership roles, including command of the 89th Reconnaissance Squadron at McChord Field, Washington. These assignments provided him with diverse experiences that would prove invaluable in the years to come.

The late 1930s and early 1940s were marked by significant advancements in military aviation technology. New aircraft designs, improved navigation systems, and enhanced air combat tactics were being developed, and John was at the forefront of these innovations. His expertise in mechanical engineering and as a pilot made him well-suited to contribute to these developments.

One of the most defining moments in the career of John Hilger was his participation in the Doolittle Raid. John, then a major, volunteered for the mission and was selected as deputy commander. His responsibilities included training the volunteer crews, overseeing the planning and execution of the attack, and ensuring the success of the mission.

On 18 April 1942, the mission began. Having been spotted by Japanese picket boats, the B-25s had to launch earlier than planned. Despite this setback, the crews proceeded with the mission. John took off from the USS *Hornet* at 9:07 am, piloting the fourteenth bomber, with the NAA factory serial number 62B-2966 and USAAF serial number 40-2297. His assignment was to attack industrial areas and military installations in the city of Nagoya, Japan. The targets included factories, storage facilities, and other infrastructure critical to the Japanese war effort. His aircraft did not have a name.

After completing their bombing missions, the crews faced the daunting task of finding safety in China. Due to fuel shortages and navigation problems, John's crew, along with several others, were forced to bail out over China. He and his crew parachuted into Zhejiang Province, near Quzhou. They were aided by Chinese civilians and resistance fighters, who helped them evade Japanese forces and reach safety. The bravery and support of the Chinese people were crucial to their survival.

After their daring mission the Doolittle Raiders, including John, embarked on a difficult journey back to the United States. This return was filled with challenges, such as navigating through hostile territory and collaborating closely with Allied forces to ensure a safe return home.

Most of the surviving raiders, including John, returned to the United States by the summer of 1942. They were welcomed as heroes, and their return was a significant morale boost for the American public during the difficult early months of the Second World War. On 27 June 1942, John, along with other raiders, was awarded the Distinguished Flying Cross by General Hap Arnold at Bolling Field, Washington, D.C. This award recognized his bravery and leadership during the raid. The Doolittle Raid cemented John's reputation as a courageous and capable officer.

The return of the Doolittle Raiders and the subsequent recognition were significant moments in American history and symbolized the resilience and determination of the nation in times of adversity. For John, this experience marked one of the most meaningful achievements in his military career.

After the Doolittle Raid, John continued to serve in various capacities during the Second World War. His leadership skills and experience were recognized with a promotion to colonel in September 1942, and he assumed command of the 320th Bomb Group at MacDill Field, Florida. This group, equipped with B-26 Marauder bombers, played a crucial role in the Allied bombing campaigns, and John's leadership was instrumental in training and preparing the group for combat operations.

In the China-Burma-India theater, Hilger served with the 14th Air Force in Kunming, China, from July to October 1943. As commander of the Operational Training Unit Bomb Group, his role was to train Chinese and American pilots and coordinate joint operations. Due to his participation in the Doolittle Raid, however, John was forbidden from flying combat missions, for fear of his possible capture and execution by the Japanese.

During the final months of the Second World War, John served in the western Pacific as a special planning officer on the staff of Admiral Chester Nimitz, the commander-in-chief of the Pacific Ocean Areas. In this role, Hilger contributed to the strategic planning and execution of critical operations in the Pacific, including the planning for major battles such as the Battle of Okinawa. His experience and expertise were invaluable in shaping Allied strategy and ensuring the success of their operations.

After the Second World War, the United States faced new challenges, including the onset of the Cold War. John played an important role in this transition, serving in various positions within the newly established U.S. Air Force. His assignments included leadership positions in strategic planning, training, and operational testing.

From 1946 to 1948, John was stationed at the Pentagon, where he worked on the development of policies and strategies for the Air Force. His expertise in air operations and strategic planning made him a valuable asset in shaping the direction of the Air Force in its early years. John's contributions during this period helped establish the Air Force as a separate and independent branch of the U.S. military.

In 1948, John attended the Air War College at Maxwell AFB, Alabama, where he further refined his strategic and leadership skills. This education prepared him for higher command positions, including his leadership of the 306th Bomb Group at MacDill AFB and the 307th Bomb Group, which was deployed to Kadena AB, Okinawa, during the Korean War. John's service during the Korean War was marked by significant achievements, including commanding bombing missions and contributing to the strategic goals of the Air Force in the region.

In the 1950s and 1960s, John continued to serve in senior positions, including as commander of the Air Force Operational Test Center at Eglin AFB, Florida. In this role, he oversaw the testing and evaluation of new aircraft and technologies, ensuring that the Air Force maintained its technological edge during the Cold War. John's work contributed to the development and deployment of advanced aircraft and weapons systems that were crucial in maintaining the United States' military superiority.

John's career reached its peak with his appointment as chief of staff of the Allied Air Forces in northern Europe in Oslo, Norway, from 1959 to 1961. In this role, he was responsible for coordinating air operations and planning with NATO allies, ensuring a united and effective response to potential threats. His leadership and diplomatic skills were crucial in fostering cooperation and strengthening the alliance.

From 1961 to 1964, John served as chief of staff of the Air Training Command at Randolph AFB, Texas. In this role, he oversaw the training and preparation of Air Force personnel, ensuring that they were ready to meet the challenges of the Cold War. His efforts contributed to the development of a highly trained and capable Air Force.

From July 1964 until his retirement on 30 November 1966, John served as deputy chief of staff for LIVE OAK, a secret planning staff responsible for maintaining the air and land corridors between West Germany and West Berlin. This role was critical during the Cold War, as the Berlin corridors were a flashpoint for potential conflict between the Western powers and the Soviet Union. John's work ensured that the United States and its allies were prepared to respond to any threat to the access routes to Berlin.

After his retirement from the Air Force, Brigadier General John A. Hilger transitioned to a civilian career. He worked with the United States Atomic Energy Commission, contributing to the development and management of the nation's nuclear energy and weapons' program. His work in this role reflected his continued dedication to national security and technological advancement.

Throughout his life, John received numerous awards and honors, reflecting his exceptional service and accomplishments. These included the Distinguished Flying Cross, the Legion of Merit, and other military decorations. His contributions to the U.S. military, particularly his involvement in the Doolittle Raid, left a lasting legacy.

Brigadier General John A. Hilger passed away on 3 February 1982 in San Antonio, Texas, at the age of 73. In accordance with his wishes, his remains were cremated, and his ashes were scattered in the Pacific Ocean off the coast of Newport Beach, California. His death marked the end of a remarkable life, characterized by service, courage, and dedication to his country.

The achievements of Brigadier General John A. Hilger are still recognized by military historians, veterans, and those who study the significant events of the Second World War and the Cold War. He is remembered as one of five Doolittle Raiders who achieved the rank of general, alongside James H. "Jimmy" Doolittle, David M. Jones, Everett W. Holstrom, and Richard A. Knobloch. These men embodied the courage and leadership that defined their generation and left an indelible mark on military history.

John's contributions to military aviation, strategic planning, and leadership have had a lasting impact on the U.S. Air Force and the broader military community. His story is also a testament to the values of perseverance, dedication, and service. His life journey, from a boy in a small town in Sherman, Texas, to a highly respected military leader, is an inspiring tale of commitment and achievement.

As we remember Brigadier General John A. Hilger, we honor not only his individual achievements but also the collective contributions of his generation. Their efforts and sacrifices have shaped the world we live in today, ensuring the freedoms and security we often take for granted. His life and career embody the spirit of service and the unwavering commitment to duty that define the best of the U.S. military.

Pilot of Crew 15

Captain Donald G. Smith

Captain Donald Gregory "Don" Smith was born on 15 January 1918 in Oldham, South Dakota, a small town located in the vast prairies of eastern South Dakota. The environment in which Don grew up was characterized by rugged natural beauty and the challenges of rural life. Oldham was known for its wide-open spaces, harsh winters, and a tight-knit farming community. These elements played an important role in Don's early years, where he developed a strong work ethic, a deep connection to the land, and a sense of responsibility.

Don was the second son of Charles Levi Gregory and Eva Emmeline Streeter. Charles was a dedicated farmer, continuing the traditions of his ancestors who had settled in the Midwest. Farming in the early twentieth century was not without challenges: unpredictable weather, economic downturns, and the physical demands of the work. Despite these difficulties, Charles worked tirelessly to provide for his family, embodying the resilience and determination characteristic of rural life in the Midwest.

Eva, born in June 1892, was the heart of the Gregory household. She was known for her caring nature, which provided a stable and loving environment for her children. Eva's role in the family was central, as she managed the household with grace and care, ensuring her children were raised with strong values and a sense of security.

The life of the Gregory family was simple, but deeply rooted in the values of hard work, integrity, and community. Don and his siblings were taught the importance of these principles from a young age. The children were expected to contribute to the farm's activities and learned the skills necessary to help their father with daily chores. These early experiences on the farm would later shape Don's character, teaching him the importance of perseverance, discipline, and self-reliance.

However, the peaceful lifestyle of the Gregory family was soon disrupted by a global crisis. The influenza pandemic of 1918–19, which claimed millions of lives worldwide, reached even the remote areas of South Dakota. This pandemic was particularly devastating as it affected people of all ages and backgrounds. Tragically, Eva also fell victim to the disease and passed away on 13 April 1923, at the age of 30. Don was only 5 years old at the time, and the loss of his mother was a devastating blow to the family. Her death left a void in the Gregory household, and Charles was left to care for their four young children alone.

Eva Gregory's death marked the beginning of a difficult period for the family. Charles, who had to manage both the farm and the responsibility of raising his children, became overwhelmed by the daily tasks. The economic pressures of the 1920s, combined with the personal loss, made it increasingly difficult for him to continue running the farm and care for his children. Seeking a fresh start and better opportunities, Charles decided to leave Oldham and look for work in other parts of the region. This decision marked the beginning of a challenging and uncertain chapter in Don's life.

Struggling to cope with his grief and the demands of single parenthood, Charles made the heart-wrenching decision to place 6-year-old Donald and his younger sister, Grace, in the Children's Home Society orphanage in Sioux Falls, South Dakota, on 2 September 1924, without informing the extended family.

Life in the orphanage was a stark contrast to the warmth of the Gregory home. Separated from his family and struggling to understand why his father had left him, Donald faced feelings of abandonment and uncertainty. The institution's rigid structure offered little comfort, yet Donald's innate resilience began to surface. He found solace in helping younger children and excelling in his studies, building the foundation of a strength that would serve him well in the future.

A remarkable turn of events came when two of Donald's cousins, who were students at South Dakota State College, visited the orphanage. During their visit, they recognized Donald and were shocked to see him there. They immediately informed the family of his situation, prompting swift action to rescue him. On 11 January 1925, Donald and Grace were placed in the care of their uncle, Clarence Delbert Streeter, Eva's eldest brother.

Later, Donald was officially adopted by Arthur W. Smith. Veterinarian Arthur Smith's decision to provide a loving and stable home for him reflects his unwavering commitment to family and his compassionate nature. By bringing Donald back into the family fold, he not only ensured his immediate needs were met, but also laid the foundation for his emotional and psychological wellbeing. This act of selflessness likely had a profound and lasting impact on their lives, embodying the essence of what it means to prioritize love and care above all else. Donald often reflected on the significant role they played in his life, crediting them with instilling the values of hard work, determination, and perseverance.

Shortly thereafter, arrangements were made for Don and Grace's adoption. On 16 February 1925 formal adoption proceedings were initiated for Don, and by 30 June the adoption was finalized; his name was legally changed to Donald Gregory Smith and he officially became the adopted son of Arthur W. Smith.

In 1927, the family moved to Belle Fourche, a small town in the Black Hills region of South Dakota. Belle Fourche, with its rich history as a center for cattle drives and its picturesque beauty, became the backdrop for Don's formative years. The town, known for its strong sense of community and deep-rooted traditions, welcomed the Smith family, and Don soon became an active member of the local community. He was known for his friendly nature, willingness to help others, and his growing sense of responsibility. The stability and support he received from the Smiths played a crucial role in his development and allowed him to overcome the challenges of his early childhood.

Arthur Smith's profession as a veterinarian had a significant influence on Don. Arthur often took Don with him during his rounds, where the young boy learned about caring for animals and the responsibilities of veterinary medicine. This experience sparked Don's interest in livestock, particularly in raising chickens. The Smith family encouraged Don's curiosity and supported his interests, allowing him to grow up in a loving environment that was a stark contrast to his earlier experiences.

Don attended Belle Fourche High School, where he quickly excelled both academically and athletically. He was a dedicated student, known for his strong work ethic and commitment to his studies. But it was on the athletic field that Don truly shone. He participated in football, basketball, and track, excelling in each sport and earning the respect of his coaches and peers.

In football, Don played as a center, a position that required both physical strength and strategic thinking. His performances on the field were consistently impressive, and he became a key figure for his high school team. His leadership qualities and athletic ability made him a standout among his peers, and he graduated in 1936 with a reputation as a hardworking and dedicated student-athlete.

Don's athletic achievements were a source of pride for the Smith family and the entire Belle Fourche community. His success on the sports field was seen as a reflection of his character: strong, resilient, and determined. These qualities would later serve him well in his military career, where physical endurance and mental toughness were essential.

In addition to his athletic achievements, Don was also involved in other aspects of school life. He participated in student government, where he refined his leadership skills and developed a sense of civic duty. His involvement in various school clubs and organizations demonstrated his commitment to making the most of his high school experience. These early leadership roles gave him the confidence and skills that would later be crucial in his military career.

After graduating from high school, Don enrolled at the University of South Dakota. His time at the university was marked by both academic success and athletic achievement. Don continued to excel in his studies and became a standout player on the university's American football team. Playing as a center, Don's performance on the field was remarkable, earning him a spot as a Small College All-American in 1939, a prestigious honor that highlighted his skills and dedication.

In addition to his accomplishments on the football field, Don was also deeply involved in the university's Reserve Officers Training Corps program. As a cadet, Don demonstrated exceptional commitment and a strong sense of duty. His participation in the ROTC program was not only a pathway to a military commission but also a testament to his desire to serve his country.

The ROTC program at the University of South Dakota provided Don with rigorous military training that complemented his academic efforts. He learned the fundamentals of military science, leadership, and tactics, all of which were crucial for his later military career. The program also gave him a sense of camaraderie with his fellow cadets, many of whom would later serve alongside him during the Second World War.

In 1940, Don earned his Bachelor of Science degree and was commissioned as a second lieutenant in the United States Army Infantry. This achievement marked the beginning of a distinguished military career that would define much of his life. His academic success, combined with his ROTC training, prepared him well for the challenges he would face as an officer in the U.S. Army.

During his university years, Don developed a keen interest in the rapidly evolving field of aviation. This interest was strongly influenced by Clyde Ice, a legendary pilot and flight instructor from Spearfish, South Dakota. Clyde Ice was a pioneer in American aviation, known for his contributions to the development of flight training techniques and his role in promoting aviation in the region.

Clyde Ice's aviation career began in the early 1920s, and he quickly gained a reputation for his skill and daring as a pilot. He was involved in numerous aviation feats, including barnstorming, mail flights, and aerial photography. By the time Don met him, Clyde Ice had already established himself as a respected flight instructor and mentor to many aspiring pilots.

Don was introduced to Clyde Ice through mutual acquaintances in the Belle Fourche and Spearfish area. Ice recognized Don's passion and potential and took him under his wing, where he provided flying lessons and shared his extensive knowledge of aviation. Under Ice's mentorship, Don quickly demonstrated an aptitude for flying. His natural talent, combined with Ice's expert guidance, set him on a path to becoming a skilled pilot.

The relationship between Don and Clyde Ice was more than that of student and instructor; it was a partnership based on mutual respect and a shared love of aviation. Ice's influence on Don was profound: he not only taught him the technical skills necessary to operate an aircraft but also gave him the confidence and determination to pursue a career in military aviation. Ice's legacy as a mentor to young pilots like Don was part of a broader effort to prepare a new generation of aviators who would serve during the Second World War.

In July 1940, inspired by his experiences with Clyde Ice, Don began his formal flight training with the U.S. Army Air Corps. His training took place at several airfields, including Oxnard Air Force Base in California and Kelly Field in Texas. The training program was rigorous and comprehensive, covering everything from basic flight maneuvers to advanced navigation and combat tactics. Don's skills as a pilot were honed during this period, and he quickly earned a reputation as a capable and reliable aviator. On 14 March 1941, he received his wings, marking the transition from student to certified military pilot.

After earning his wings, Don was assigned to the 34th Bomb Squadron of the 17th Bomb Group at Pendleton Army Airfield in Oregon. His early assignments included routine training and participation in military exercises designed to prepare the squadron for potential combat missions. Although the United States was not yet fully involved in the Second World War at the time, tensions were rising globally, and the training and preparation during this period were crucial to ensuring the military was ready for any eventuality.

The experience Don gained during these early years in the Air Corps was invaluable. He became proficient in flying various aircraft and mastered the skills necessary for both daytime and nighttime operations. His superiors took note of his abilities, and he was soon promoted to first lieutenant, a recognition of his growing expertise and leadership potential.

During his time training as a pilot in Texas, Don met Marie Crouch, a student who shared his values of hard work, dedication, and a strong sense of community. The two quickly formed a close bond, and their relationship blossomed into a deep love. After their graduation in 1940, Don and Marie were married on 21 June 1941, in Pierce, Washington, in a small, intimate ceremony attended by close friends and family.

Their marriage was built on a strong foundation of mutual respect, love, and shared ambitions. Marie, known for her kindness, supportive nature, and deep faith, stood by Don as he pursued his military career.

Together, they faced the uncertainties of a world on the brink of war, drawing strength from each other and their shared commitment to building a life together.

As the Second World War intensified, Don's military obligations became increasingly demanding. In early 1942, following the attack on Pearl Harbor, Don volunteered for the Doolittle Raid. The couple were aware of the risks involved in the mission, and Marie, who was pregnant with their first child, was both proud and anxious as Don prepared for this significant operation.

The bond between Don and Marie was a source of comfort and strength for both during these challenging times. Despite the uncertainties and dangers of war, they remained devoted to each other and to the family they were building. Marie's unwavering support was a crucial factor in Don's ability to focus on his military duties, knowing that his family stood by him every step of the way.

The selection process for the Doolittle Raid was highly competitive, with only the most skilled and dedicated pilots chosen. Don's selection for the mission was a testament to his abilities as a pilot and his willingness to undertake a dangerous and uncertain mission for his country. The intense training regimen at Eglin Field was designed to prepare the crews for the unique challenges they would face, including the unprecedented task of launching a B-25 bomber from the deck of an aircraft carrier.

The training also included extensive briefings on the strategic importance of the mission and the potential risks involved. The volunteers were fully aware that their chances of returning safely were slim, but their commitment to the mission never wavered. For Don, the opportunity to strike back at the enemy that had attacked Pearl Harbor was a powerful motivation, and he approached the mission with a sense of duty and determination.

On 2 April 1942, the USS *Hornet* set sail with sixteen B-25 bombers, including Don's aircraft, codenamed "TNT," with USAAF serial number 40-2267 and the manufacturer's serial number 62B-2936. On 18 April the decision was made to launch the bombers immediately, even though they were still many miles from the intended launch point.

The Doolittle Raid was carried out with remarkable precision and bravery. Don and his crew, designated as Crew 15, took off from the *Hornet* at 9:15 am and headed toward Tokyo. The raid inflicted damage on key industrial and military targets and sent a clear message to Japan. However, the real challenge began after the bombings, as the crews faced the daunting task of reaching China with limited fuel and worsening weather conditions.

Don expertly piloted his aircraft toward the Chinese coastline. As they neared land, it became clear that their fuel reserves were critically low. In a remarkable feat of piloting, Don executed a perfect water landing off the coast of Tantou Mountain Island in Zhejiang Province. The crew safely exited the aircraft, but rough seas quickly separated them. Despite the difficult conditions, the crew survived the night, clinging to an inflatable life raft and some debris.

The stranded crew encountered a local farmer named Ma Liangshui, who, along with his family, provided crucial assistance. Despite the risks of Japanese patrols, the family hid the American airmen, provided them with food and dry clothes, and eventually helped them escape by disguising them as local fishermen. The bravery and hospitality of the Chinese villagers were vital in ensuring the crew's survival during this dangerous period.

The raid had been successful in terms of psychological impact, but the journey to safety was far from over. Led by Chinese resistance fighters, Don and his crew navigated through Japanese-occupied territory and eventually reached the safety of inland China.

After the perilous journey through China, Don and his surviving crew members eventually returned to the United States. Upon his return, he was hailed as a hero. The Doolittle Raid had captured the public's imagination, and the participants were celebrated for their courage and daring. Don received a hero's welcome at his university in Brookings, South Dakota. This return to his alma mater was a proud event for both himself and the community that had supported him throughout his military career. The university recognized his bravery and the crucial role he had played in one of the most daring missions of the Second World War.

In addition to the honors he received at his university, Don was guest of honor during the 1942 Black Hills Roundup in Belle Fourche. This event was particularly meaningful for him, and he considered it the pinnacle of all the celebrations he attended. The Black Hills Roundup, an important annual rodeo and community event, provided a platform on which Don was celebrated not only as a war hero but also as a beloved member of his local community.

These events reflected the immense pride and admiration that the people of South Dakota and the broader American public felt for Don and his fellow Doolittle Raiders. His presence at these celebrations served as an inspiration to many and highlighted the sacrifices made by military personnel during the war.

Don then eagerly prepared for the next phase of his life. His wife, Marie, was pregnant and was due to give birth soon. In a fortunate turn of events, Don was able to be present at the hospital when Marie gave birth to their daughter, Donna, on 6 June 1942. The birth of Donna was a profoundly joyful event that marked the beginning of a new chapter in their lives, in the midst of the ongoing war.

Becoming a father was a significant milestone in Don's life, representing the continuity of life and the hope for a better future, even during wartime. It added new dimension to his sense of duty and responsibility, reinforcing his commitment to fight for the freedoms that would ensure a safe and secure world for his daughter.

Despite the accolades and recognition following the Doolittle Raid, Don knew that his service was far from over. He was reassigned to the 439th Bomb Squadron of the 319th Bomb Group, where he was trained to fly the B-26 Marauder. The B-26 was a fast and versatile medium bomber that required precise handling and pilot skills. Don's training at Barksdale Field in Louisiana was intense and included advanced flight techniques, bombing strategies, and formation flying. He quickly adapted to the new aircraft and became one of the most capable pilots in the squadron.

In September 1942, Don was deployed to England as part of the Allied buildup in preparation for Operation Torch, the Allied invasion of French North Africa. He was stationed at RAF Attlebridge, near Norwich in Norfolk, a key base for the U.S. Air Force in Europe. The mission was to support the invasion by bombing Axis supply lines, airfields, and military installations.

On 12 November 1942, Captain Donald G. Smith embarked on what would be his final mission. Tragically, Don's B-26 Marauder, on a flight from RAF Attlebridge to St Eval, crashed near Abbots Ripton at approximately 3:00 pm due to poor weather conditions. He did not survive the crash. The crash itself underscores the dangerous nature of military training sessions during the Second World War, where pilots not only had to face the perils of combat, but also the risks posed by challenging weather conditions and flying circumstances.

The news of Don's death was a devastating blow to his family and comrades. His loss was deeply felt by everyone who knew him, especially by Marie, who was left to raise their daughter Donna alone. Don's death underscored the harsh realities of war and the high price paid by those who served.

The death of Captain Donald Smith was a great loss to his family, friends, and the military community. He was remembered as a brave and skilled pilot, a dedicated officer, and a compassionate individual. His actions during the Doolittle Raid and subsequent missions embodied the courage and dedication of those who served during the Second World War.

In recognition of his service and sacrifice, Captain Donald G. Smith was posthumously inducted into the South Dakota Hall of Fame in 2004. This honor reflected the high regard in which he was held and the lasting impact of his contributions.

The legacy of Captain Donald Gregory "Don" Smith is preserved not only in the official records of the Doolittle Raid and the Second World War, but also in the hearts and minds of those who knew him. His story is one of perseverance, courage, and an unwavering commitment to his country. The sacrifices he made, both on the battlefield and in his personal life, serve as a powerful reminder of the cost of freedom and the indomitable spirit of those who fight to protect it.

In addition to his induction into the South Dakota Hall of Fame, Don's memory is honored by various memorials and tributes. His name is engraved on the Doolittle Raiders Memorial, and his story is told in numerous books, documentaries, and historical accounts of the Second World War. These tributes ensure that future generations will remember and appreciate the sacrifices of Don and his fellow airmen.

Marie and Donna remained in South Dakota after the war and kept Don's memory alive through their stories and the values he had instilled in them. Marie, in particular, remained an active member of the community, sharing Don's story with others to ensure that his legacy would not be forgotten.

Today, the story of Captain Donald G. "Don" Smith serves as a lasting example of what it means to serve one's country with honor and integrity. His legacy lives on in the hearts of his family, the annals of military history, and the collective memory of a grateful nation. Captain Donald G. "Don" Smith is buried at Pine Slope Cemetery in Belle Fourche, South Dakota. His grave serves as a lasting memorial to his courage and sacrifice, ensuring that his legacy lives on in the community he called home.

Don Smith had two sisters and one brother. Don's sister, Dorothy, lived to the age of 103 and passed away in 2019. At the age of 7, she lost her mother, who was also Don's mother, after which she and her siblings were separated. Don was sent to an orphanage, while Dorothy was adopted by their aunt and uncle, William and Helen Streeter. His other sister, Grace, born in 1923, died in 2009. Don's older brother, George, born in 1914, died in 1982.

Don's adoptive father, Arthur Smith, was so devastated by the loss of his adopted son that he passed away a few weeks after Don's death, on 24 December 1942. His adoptive mother, Laura Bolte, died in 1964. Don's biological father, Charles Levi Gregory, died in 1967.

Pilot of Crew 16

Lieutenant William G. Farrow

Lieutenant William Glover "Bill" Farrow was born on 24 September 1918, in Darlington, South Carolina, a small yet vibrant town known for its agricultural roots and tight-knit community. Darlington thrived on the values of hard work, respect, and a strong sense of duty, which were deeply ingrained in Southern culture. These values shaped William's character from a young age. Growing up in a community where neighbors looked out for each other and perseverance was key, William developed the traits of resilience and responsibility that would later define him during his military career.

William was the eldest child of Isaac Glover Farrow and Jessie May Stem. His father, born on 25 December 1889, grew up in a modest family and found work in the tobacco industry, a major economic sector in the southern United States in the early twentieth century. He worked long hours in a cigarette factory in Raleigh, North Carolina, and despite the harsh conditions, this job provided stability for the family. Isaac's determination to support his family became an important example for William.

William's mother, Jessie May Stem, born on 16 February 1893, came from a wealthier family involved in the tobacco trade. Her family owned a tobacco warehouse, which was a lucrative business at the time. Jessie grew up in relative comfort and had access to a good education. Despite her privileged upbringing, she developed a strong bond with Isaac, based on shared values of hard work, respect, and family. Jessie easily adapted to a simpler life and played a crucial role in raising their children. Her patience, grace, and determination left a deep impression on William.

The Farrow family adhered to strict moral values, with integrity, hard work, and respect for others at the core. These principles were the foundation of William's upbringing and remained a guiding force throughout his life, both privately and later in his military career. When William was still young, the family moved to Darlington, South Carolina, known for its strong sense of community, rooted in Southern traditions of agriculture and family values. In this environment, William was raised with principles such as honesty, responsibility, and caring for others.

In Darlington, William developed a strong sense of responsibility and a deep awareness of duty. His parents taught him that hard work and honesty were far more important than material wealth or social status. These values greatly influenced his behavior and personal life. As a child, William already showed great curiosity and fascination with the world around him. He was eager to learn and always sought to understand how things worked. His parents encouraged this curiosity and motivated him to explore his interests. He soon developed a deep interest in technology and mechanics, always wanting to know how things were constructed and functioned.

One of the most influential factors in William's childhood was his growing passion for aviation. From an early age, he became fascinated by stories of aviation pioneers and the brave pilots of the First World War, who flew into the sky in their fragile planes. These stories left a deep impression on him and inspired him to pursue his dream: to become a pilot and take to the skies.

William began his schooling at Washington Street Elementary School in Darlington, a simple school with one classroom where children of different ages were taught together. Despite the school's limited resources, William quickly excelled in his studies. He had a sharp intellect and was always eager to learn more. His teachers recognized his potential and encouraged him to take his studies seriously. Thanks to his intelligence and determination, William often ranked as the top student in his class.

At the age of 11, William faced a major change in his life. His parents' marriage came under pressure due to his father's personal problems, including alcoholism and infidelity. These tensions eventually led to a divorce, an event that had a significant impact on William and his younger sister, Marjorie. In the early twentieth century, divorce was still rare and often carried a social stigma. For William, the divorce meant not only the loss of his family's stability but also a change in his living environment. William, his sister, and his mother left Darlington for a while. However, after the divorce, William and his mother returned to Darlington, where they tried to build a new life. His younger sister Marjorie remained with Jessie's parents, who raised her in a more stable environment.

Despite the turbulent personal circumstances, William remained focused on his studies and his future plans. He found comfort in his schoolwork and his love of books. His ability to persevere during difficult times demonstrated his resilience and determination, qualities that would later prove valuable in his military career.

After the divorce, William's mother, Jessie, found work at the McFall Hotel in Darlington, owned by her uncle, Harold McFall. This job not only provided her with financial stability but also offered housing for her and William. They were given an apartment in the hotel, which became their home for the coming years. Living in a hotel offered William a unique experience. The McFall Hotel was always lively, with guests constantly checking in and out. This dynamic environment gave William the opportunity to interact with people from different walks of life, each with their own stories and backgrounds. William enjoyed listening to the experiences of the guests, which broadened his worldview and gave him a wider perspective on life.

Additionally, life in the hotel also provided William with practical lessons about discipline and responsibility. He watched as his mother managed the hotel with iron discipline and a keen eye for detail. Her work ethic and dedication made a deep impression on him and inspired him to apply the same dedication in his own life.

After his elementary school years, William attended Darlington Junior High School and later St John's High School, where he continued to stand out for his academic achievements and leadership qualities. He was a popular student, both for his intelligence and his willingness to help others. William had a natural talent for leadership, which became evident through his involvement in various school activities. He often took on the responsibility of guiding and supporting his fellow students in their studies.

His teachers recognized his academic talent and encouraged him to further develop his intellect. Although William excelled in the classroom and was encouraged to pursue a career in science or engineering, his true passion remained aviation. His fascination with airplanes, pilots, and the technical aspects of flying continued to dominate his thoughts. During his high school years, William read everything he could find about aviation and dreamed of becoming a pilot himself. His love for aviation was more than just an interest; it became his calling. He was determined to fulfill his dream and take to the skies himself.

In the 1920s and 1930s, aviation was a relatively new but exciting technology. The era witnessed the daring feats of aviation pioneers such as Charles Lindbergh, who crossed the Atlantic solo in 1927, and Amelia Earhart, who in 1928 became the first female pilot to achieve the feat. These adventures inspired a whole generation, including William, to dream of a career in aviation.

William's curiosity about the mechanics of airplanes also led him to delve into how airplanes were built and maintained. He didn't just want to fly; he wanted to understand how the machines worked. His interest in both the technical and operational aspects of aviation fueled his desire to pursue a career in the field.

In 1935, after graduating from St John's High School, William continued his education at the University of Southern California (USC). Once again, he excelled academically while continuing to nurture his passion for aviation. In 1939, he was selected by the Civil Aeronautics Authority as one of three USC students for a government-sponsored pilot training program. This prestigious program offered William the opportunity to receive formal flight training at the Hawthorne School of Aeronautics in Orangeburg, South Carolina.

After months of intensive training, William earned his pilot's license in March 1940. Shortly thereafter, as the world stood on the brink of war, William was called to report to Love Field in Dallas, Texas. In November 1940, he officially joined the U.S. Army Air Corps (USAAC) through the Aviation Cadet Program, marking the beginning of the military phase of his career.

In February 1941, William was transferred to the San Angelo Air Corps Basic Flying School in Texas, where he underwent intensive flight training. This training emphasized both technical flying skills and leadership. After completing his training, William was officially commissioned as a lieutenant in the USAAC in July 1941. He specialized in flying the B-25 Mitchell, the medium bomber that would later play a crucial role in the war. Shortly after his commission, William was assigned to the 34th Bomb Squadron at Pendleton Field, Oregon.

With the rise of fascist regimes in Europe and increasing Japanese aggression in Asia, the global stage was rapidly changing. William, like many young men of his generation, felt a deep sense of duty to serve his country. Events such as Nazi Germany's annexation of Austria and invasion of Czechoslovakia made it clear that a world war was imminent. In Asia, Japan continued its expansion by conquering territories in China, leading to increasing tensions in the region.

In early 1942, William volunteered for the Doolittle Raid. Along with other members of the 17th Bombardment Group, to which his squadron belonged, he began intensive training at Eglin Field in Florida. There, they practiced taking off from short runways that simulated the deck of an aircraft carrier. This required utmost precision and concentration, as the B-25 normally took off from long runways. The training was tough and physically demanding, but William and his fellow pilots knew that the success of the mission depended entirely on their ability to overcome this challenge.

On 2 April 1942, the USS *Hornet* departed from San Francisco, loaded with sixteen B-25 bombers, including William's aircraft. At 9:19 am on 18 April, Lieutenant William G. Farrow piloted aircraft number 16, known as "Bat Out of Hell". This aircraft carried the USAAF serial number 40-2268 and the factory serial number 62B-2937. Farrow and his crew were the sixteenth and last B-25 to take off from the *Hornet*.

William and his crew reached their target on the Japanese mainland and successfully bombed their objectives. After completing the bombing mission, William and his crew faced a new problem: they had been forced to take off sooner than planned after being spotted by a Japanese picket boat, and so the planes did not have enough fuel to reach the planned landing sites in China. The crews had to improvise and hope for an emergency landing in China. As William and his crew neared the Chinese coast, they realized they had no choice but to bail out of the aircraft. They parachuted out near Nanchang, in Japanese-occupied China, hoping for a safe landing.

However, the crew of "Bat Out of Hell" soon encountered hostile soldiers and difficult terrain. Although they tried to contact Chinese allies, William and his crewmembers were eventually captured by Japanese forces.

After their capture, William and his crew were taken to Shanghai, China, where they were interrogated by Japanese military authorities. The Japanese, furious about the attack on their capital and other cities, sought every possible piece of information from the prisoners. William and his crew were subjected to torture in an attempt to extract strategic information about American military operations. Despite the severe physical and mental torture, William refused to divulge sensitive information and remained steadfast.

For further interrogation, the Americans were flown to Tokyo. In the Japanese capital, they were subjected to even more intense and brutal interrogations by the Japanese military authorities, who were determined to extract as much information as possible.

The prisoners were held in deplorable conditions. They were given barely any food, lived in unsanitary conditions, and were constantly threatened with execution. Despite this brutal treatment, William maintained his dignity and encouraged his fellow prisoners to stay strong.

In August 1942, William and seven other captured Doolittle Raiders, including members of Crew 6 and Crew 7, were brought before a Japanese military court in Shanghai, where they were subjected to a sham trial. The trial was conducted entirely in Japanese and offered the prisoners no opportunity to defend themselves. The outcome was predetermined: the court sentenced them all to death.

William Farrow, along with two other prisoners, Hallmark and Spatz, was selected for immediate execution. The remaining prisoners were eventually given life sentences instead of the death penalty.

The night before their execution, the men were permitted to write final letters. The International Red Cross was to mail the letters after receiving them from the Japanese. The Japanese, however, did not pass on the letters, and they were never mailed. William wrote letters to his mother and to a friend, Lieutenant Ivan Ferguson. In the letter addressed to his mother, he wrote:

> You have given much, so much more to me than I have returned, but such is the Christian way. You are and always will be a real angel. Be brave and strong for my sake. I love you, Mom, from the depths of a full heart ... Don't let this get you down. Just remember God will make everything right and that I'll see you all again in the hereafter. ... So let me implore you to keep your chin up. Be brave and strong for my sake. P.S. My insurance policy is in my bag in a small tent in Columbia. Read *Thanatopsis* by Bryant if you want to know how I am taking this. My faith in God is complete, so I am unafraid.

On 15 October 1942, William and his two fellow prisoners were taken to a cemetery outside Shanghai, Public Cemetery No. 1. There, they were forced to kneel in front of wooden crosses, with their hands tied behind their backs. A white cloth with a black "X" was placed over their faces as a target for the firing squad. The execution was swift and merciless. William was shot, and his body was cremated.

The brutal execution of William Glover Farrow marked the tragic end of a brave young man who gave his life for his country. His death was one of many sacrifices made during the war, but his courage and determination would earn him posthumous recognition and tribute.

After the war, William's bravery was not forgotten. He was posthumously awarded several military honors, including the Distinguished Flying Cross, the Purple Heart, and the Prisoner of War Medal. In January 1949, his urn was recovered in Shanghai and reburied with full military honors at Arlington National Cemetery in Virginia. The ceremony brought a sense of closure for his family and the nation, and his courage and sacrifice became a symbol of the fight for freedom during the war.

William's story was recorded in numerous books, documentaries, and historical works about the Second World War and the Doolittle Raid. His name became an inspiration for generations of American pilots and soldiers, and his legacy lives on as a reminder of the sacrifices made for freedom.

In 1998, a remarkable discovery was made in Suffolk, England. A farmer named Michael Buckmaster found a keychain with car keys and a metal tag hanging from a tree branch. The tag bore the name "William G. Farrow" and the address "Darlington, South Carolina." No one knows exactly how the keys ended up in England, but the discovery added a mysterious chapter to William's legacy.

These keys were eventually returned to the United States and added to the collection of the Darlington County Historical Commission. They now serve as a tangible reminder of William Farrow's life and the sacrifice he made for his country.

Although William's life ended tragically at a young age, his legacy continues to live on today. His story is an example of unwavering courage, determination, and a deep sense of responsibility to his country. For the American public, the Doolittle Raid was a morale booster. It showed that, despite the devastation of Pearl Harbor, the U.S. was willing and able to fight back. For William Farrow and the other Doolittle Raiders, it was not just a military operation, but a symbolic gesture illustrating the courage of the American armed forces.

William G. Farrow's legacy has become an inspiration for many. His brave actions during the Doolittle Raid and his steadfastness as a prisoner of war demonstrate the resolve of a young man who risked his life for the freedom of his country. Although hc lost his life at the age of only 24, his story has left a lasting impact on generations after him, both inside and outside the military.

Farrow's legacy has also left a deep impression within the U.S. Air Force. After his death, he became a symbol of courage and duty. His story has been used to inspire later generations of pilots, not only for his bravery during the raid itself but also for his steadfastness as a prisoner of war. The U.S. Air Force Academy commemorates the Doolittle Raiders annually, and William Glover Farrow's name is mentioned alongside his fellow heroes.

His courage was further honored by Air Force units dedicated to keeping the values of determination and sacrifice alive. William's story is told to new recruits as a reminder of the sacrifices made for their freedom and as an example of how duty to country and freedom must come before everything, even in the most difficult and dangerous circumstances.

In Darlington, South Carolina, the town where William grew up, his legacy is also cherished. The Darlington County Historical Commission has done everything it can to keep his story alive. The museum holds some of William's personal belongings, including letters and photos, and organizes annual commemorations for the local heroes who gave their lives in the war.

The community in Darlington has also found other ways to honor William's memory. William G. Farrow Park was opened as a lasting tribute to his life and service. The park not only provides a place of relaxation for the local population but also serves as a memorial to his bravery. Each year, residents and veterans gather to reflect on the sacrifices made during the war and to remember local heroes like William.

Farrow's story is also an example of human resilience and the ability to maintain dignity, even in the most dire circumstances. His refusal to give sensitive information to the enemy, even under torture, shows his commitment to his country and his fellow soldiers. It reminds us that true courage is often shown in the hardest moments, when it would be easiest to give up.

For the Farrow family, William's tragic death remained a source of pain, but also of pride. His parents, Isaac and Jessie, saw their son grow into a national hero. After his death, William was honored with military awards, but his loss remained a personal tragedy for them. William's reburial at Arlington brought the family some comfort, as his sacrifice was recognized by the American people and government. His grave, located among other heroes of the Second World War, serves as a permanent reminder of his courage.

Today, William Glover Farrow remains a symbol of heroism. His story has inspired many, from historians to filmmakers, and it continues to be an integral part of American war folklore. For the people of Darlington, he is a local hero, whose name is carried with pride. For the United States, he is one of many young men who gave their lives for freedom, but his unique courage and determination make him a special figure in the history of the Second World War.

The car keys found in England add an extra mysterious chapter to his legacy. These symbols of his life were eventually returned to his homeland as a reminder of his long journey and his final return home, in the hearts and memories of those who continue to tell his story.

William Glover Farrow remains, to this day, a source of inspiration and a reminder of the courage needed to defend freedom, even in the most hopeless situations. His legacy will continue to live on as an example of what it means to place duty and honor above all else.

Sources

Primary Sources

Doolittle, James H. (1942). General Doolittle's report on the raid, written on 9 July 1942.

Joyce, Richard O., with Samuel Van Pelt. (1995). "You Bet I Was Scared: A Doolittle Raider Remembers." *Nebraska History*, 76: 54–65. Interview by Samuel Van Pelt.

Lawson, Ted W. (1943). *Thirty Seconds Over Tokyo*. Random House.

Personal accounts from the website *Children of the Doolittle Raiders*, including recollections of Lt. Colonel Mac McElroy by Donna McElroy-Hatch.

Books on the Doolittle Raid

Chun, Clayton. (2006). *Doolittle Raid 1942: America's First Strike Back at Japan*. Osprey Publishing. Van Nostrand.

Glines, Carroll V. (1964). *Doolittle's Tokyo Raiders*. Princeton, N.J.: Van Nostrand.

Glines, Carroll V. (1964). *The Doolittle Tokyo Raiders*. Van Nostrand.

Glines, Carroll V. (1988). *Echoes of the Doolittle Raid*. Schiffer Publishing.

Glines, Carroll V. (1988). *The Doolittle Raid: The Mission that Changed the War*. Orion Books.

Glines, Carroll V. (1990). *The Doolittle Raid: America's Daring First Strike Against Japan*. Schiffer Publishing.

Glines, Carroll V. (1995). *Four Came Home*. Pictorial Histories Publishing.

Lukacs, John D. (2010). *The Tokyo Raid: The First Doolittle Attack.* Simon & Schuster.

Martin, Michael. (2018). *Doolittle's Tokyo Raiders: The Legendary Attack on Japan That Changed the Course of World War II.* CreateSpace Independent Publishing Platform.

Nelson, Craig. (2002). *The First Heroes: The Extraordinary Story of the Doolittle Raid – America's First World War II Victory*. Penguin.

O'Keefe, James W. (2008). *The Other Doolittle Raid: The Rescue Mission After the Bombing of Tokyo*. Self-published.

O'Keefe, James W. *Bombing of Tokyo*. Self Published.

Rottiers, Geert. (2023). *Brave Young Men*. Self Published.

Rottiers, Geert. (2024). *De Onmogelijke Vlucht*. Het Punt.

Bombing of Tokyo. Self Published.

Scott, James M. (2015). *Target Tokyo: Jimmy Doolittle and the Raid That Avenged Pearl Harbor*. W.W. Norton & Company.

Biographical and Personal Accounts

Greening, Ross. (1948). *Not as Briefed: From the Doolittle Raid to a German Stalag*. Edited by Karen Morgan Driscoll and Dorothy Greening. WSU Press.

Higbee, Paul. (2005). *The First Strike: Doolittle Raider Donald Smith*. SDSH Press.

Hoppes, Jonna Doolittle. (2005). *Jimmy Doolittle: Daredevil Aviator and Scientist*. Santa Monica Press.

Paradis, Michel. (2020). *Last Mission to Tokyo: The Extraordinary Story of the Doolittle Raiders and Their Final Fight for Justice*. Simon & Schuster.

Nolta, George. (2018). *The Doolittle Raiders – What Heroes Do after the War.* Schiffer Publishing.

Meadows Stem, Margaret. (1966). *Tall and Free as Meant by God.* Carlton Press.

Tillman, Barrett. (2017). *Jimmy Doolittle: The Commander Behind the Legend.* Regenery History.

Historical Analyses and Additional Works

Lawson, Robert L. (2002). *Target Tokyo: The Story of the Doolittle Raid.* Schiffer Publishing.

Smith, Douglas V. (2010). *The Doolittle Raid and the Battle of the Coral Sea.* Naval Institute Press.

Stillwell, Paul. (2013). *Doolittle's Tokyo Raiders: The Extraordinary Story of the First American Attack on Japan.* Smithsonian Books.

Wukovits, John F. (2013). *Jimmy Doolittle: American Aviator.* Palgrave Macmillan.

Warren L. Wise. (2022). "Article on William Farrow" *Post and Courier* in Charleston, South Carolina.

Online Resources

Together We Served – https://www.togetherweserved.com/

The Doolittle Raid – https://www.doolittle-raid.net

Wikipedia, several Wikipedia pages.

FamilySearch – https://www.familysearch.org/en/united-states/

Find a Grave – https://www.findagrave.com/

The Hall of Valour Project – https://valor.militarytimes.com/

Several websites of cities and municipalities in the USA.

Various online newspapers that feature interviews and articles about the pilots who flew in the Doolittle Raid.

Various websites that contain the obituaries of the former pilots of the Doolittle Raid.

Facebook page The Doolittle Raid. – https://www.facebook.com/profile.php?id=100093570602530

The author's website www.doolittle-raid.net occasionally posts updates about the pilots. Click on "CREWS" and then click on the respective pilot of the crew.

The Facebook page The Doolittle Raid posts daily updates also.

Use of Public Domain Photographs.

This book includes photographs that are in the public domain under United States copyright law. According to Title 17, Chapter 1, Section 105 of the U.S. Code, "[c]opyright protection under this title is not available for any work of the United States Government." As such, works created by U.S. government employees in the course of their official duties are not subject to copyright protection and are considered public domain.

The photographs included here were sourced from the collections of the National Archives and Records Administration (NARA) and other U.S. government agencies. These images, including historical photographs of the Doolittle Raid and its participants, are reproduced with the understanding that they remain free from copyright restrictions.

While these images are legally free to use, this book acknowledges and credits the original source of each photograph to maintain transparency and respect for the institutions that preserve these important historical documents. Full citations, including image identifiers and source details, are provided in the image captions and in the "Image Credits" section at the back of the book.

By utilizing these public domain resources, we aim to bring historical accuracy and visual richness to the story of the Doolittle Raid, ensuring that the legacy of these events is preserved and accessible to all.

A book is never written alone. Without the invaluable support and assistance of several exceptional people, this project would not have been possible. To them, I extend my deepest gratitude.

The editorial work was carefully undertaken by my wife, Chris, and my sons, Niels, his girlfriend Luna, and Mats. I would also like to acknowledge Najima and Boris – two people I can always count on. Their involvement means so much to me. The support of my sister Ruth, my brother Wim, and my ever-curious friends, who constantly ask what I am working on this time, has been equally indispensable.

My mother, Jeanne, who at 84 years old still passionately defends democratic values, deserves special mention. Her dedication stems from the war years her father endured. It is from her and my late father, Siegfried, that I inherited my love and fascination for the history of the Second World War.

My thanks also go to the staff at the History of Aviation Archives at the University of Texas at Dallas for their valuable assistance and expertise. I am also deeply grateful to Mervyn Roberts, PhD, history instructor, for guiding me in the right direction, offering support, and working on one of the biographies included in this book. The same gratitude extends to those who provided help, without which the biographies would not have been as informative.

Finally, I would like to thank John Grehan and Karyn Burnham, both with my publisher Pen and Sword. Two highly dedicated individuals who are always there for their authors. What professionalism!

Comments or feedback are always welcome at headquarters@doolittle-raid.net.